A LINE ABOVE THE SKY

A LINE ABOVE THE SKY

A story of mountains and motherhood

HELEN MORT

1

Ebury Press, an imprint of Ebury Publishing
20 Vauxhall Bridge Road
London SW1V 2SA

Ebury Press is part of the Penguin Random House group of companies
whose addresses can be found at global.penguinrandomhouse.com

First published by Ebury Press in 2022

www.penguin.co.uk

A CIP catalogue record for this book is available from the British Library

Hardback ISBN 9781529107784
Trade paperback ISBN 9781529149180

Printed and bound in Great Britain by Clays Ltd, Elcograf S.p.A.

The authorised representative in the EEA is Penguin Random House Ireland,
Morrison Chambers, 32 Nassau Street, Dublin D02 YH68

for Mum and Dad,
and for Bear

i.m Alison Hargreaves (1962–1995) and
Tom Ballard (1988–2019)

/ GEAR

It is never the right time. September, October, the valleys holding the clouds close like nursed resentments. The trees shudder, premonitions of storm. There will never be a settled day. You could wait for one all your life, palms pressed to the fogged-up windowpane, rucksack spilling its contents on the floor, the kettle singing its high, shrill song in the background.

There is no such thing as bad weather. Repeat it like a mantra. You must pack for anything. Warm layers. Waterproofs and dry socks. A head torch and spare batteries in case darkness folds over the hills faster than you imagined. A modest food supply. Prayers. Hopes. Humility. There is no such thing as bad weather, only unsuitable clothes. Packing is a comfort. There is no such thing as bad weather, only unsuitable thoughts.

Your muscles ache. As you walk, your left knee rebukes you for the poor care you've taken of it. Crows scatter from the nearest branches, flinging the ink of themselves across the morning's used page. There is no such thing as a fresh start. It will never be the right moment. You must make good progress. Leave now while you still can.

AS WELL IGNORE GRAVITY

'My life is for me. / As well ignore gravity'

– Philip Larkin

2018

High above eastern Nepal, Ama Dablam is a mother wearing a glittering necklace. This is no Romantic metaphor: it is the mountain's true name. From the trail towards Everest base camp, it dominates the eastern sky, shadows clinging to it, snow cleaving to its steepness. It is a dazzling triptych. The long ridges on each side are the arms of a mother (*ama*) protecting her child and the hanging glacier is like a double pendant (*dablam*) worn by Sherpa women. It soars dramatically, proud among the high reaches of the Himalaya. As I was giving birth to my son in December 2018, my friend, ex-boyfriend and climbing partner, Andrew, was scaling it, slow and methodical. When the contractions gripped my whole body, it was him I thought of unaccountably, him struggling through the thickness of snow and the thinness of air, climbing steadily towards a cold dawn, light breaking, a sudden blush over Cho Oyu and Numbur, all the jagged peaks of the Western Himalaya. I saw him pause on the South-West Ridge, sheerness on either side of him, a gold and rusted band of sky behind. I saw him glance down to left and right, appraising the swoop of the land, then fix his eyes on the slope ahead, the distance yet to cover. No going back.

Labour had wrung my every muscle. It was electric, heavy, dizzying. The gush of waters on the bathroom floor, the gathering ache, spasms and crumpling, the buzz of the TENS machine, stinging my lower back. When I couldn't stay at home any longer, my partner Jess drove me from Sheffield through the misty, orange-lit evening to Chesterfield Royal Hospital and I fell asleep for seconds in the gaps between contractions, slipping into a temporary oblivion, waking to sharpness. The hospital is on the road I grew up on and I'd decided I wanted to give birth there, like a wounded animal crawling home. As I doubled up on the examination table in the birthing suite, I felt embarrassed: I had always thought I would endure better than this. I was a climber, a long-distance runner, an athlete used to mountain marathons and lactic acid and nausea. But I was on the cusp of advanced labour – eight centimetres dilated – and I had got there with no pain relief apart from warm baths and paracetamol. Other kinds of pain I'd felt before suddenly seemed abstract, the way my body had always forgotten the struggle of long-distance running after I'd crossed the finish line, forgotten the fear of the climb after I'd reached the top. In the relief that comes after you gain a summit, the ascent is briefly lost.

The midwife was animated, energetic. I was given a transparent plastic nozzle attached to a long tube and I clutched it in my right hand. Outside, the sky was heavy, a premonition of snow. There were Christmas lights in the car park winking orange and green, a neon Santa on a sledge. I remembered walking round the hospital grounds one winter night on my own as a teenager, finding a bank where I could sink up to my waist in the snow, staying for hours in the privacy of the cold, my hands numb under my gloves, never wanting to go home. The midwife – Claire – talked me calmly through the method for using gas and air, explained how Entonox works, how it was important to breathe it as soon as I felt the contractions starting, how most people leave it too late. I took a tentative breath. *Deeper*, Claire said. I took a long shuddering gulp. Soon, it felt like second nature to me. My limbs tingled and my head spun. I was a climber at altitude, sucking on supplementary oxygen through a mask.

Mountains steal your breath from you. The higher you go, the thinner the air is. Air pressure at higher elevations is lower than at sea level, and oxygen molecules are squeezed tight. Within seconds of exposure to altitude, your breath quickens and your legs become leaden. Within hours, you become dehydrated and tired. If you develop altitude sickness, you become insomniac and nauseous, too lethargic to move. Most climbers who make it above 6,000 metres rely on oxygen to prevent hypoxia, though there are some who have climbed the highest mountain in the world without it, athletes like Reinhold Messner and Alison Hargreaves. But most breathe the bottled air. With their goggles and masks, they look like aliens, stumbling towards the sun. With each contraction, I inhaled more Entonox. I sank into the hot water of the birthing pool. I always kept the tube of gas and air in one hand, as if for security. It made me drunk, giddy, warm and distant. I began to hover somewhere above my own swollen body. I was following Andrew up Ama Dablam, steady and sure-footed, knowing the rope was between us. And as my body began to push of its own accord, convulsing beneath the surface of the water, I tried to take myself away to the other side of the world, to put myself in a place of ice and weather.

When I gave birth, I was overdramatic – I felt that I was fighting for my life. The moment the surgeon brought out forceps and other bright tools to perform an episiotomy, I cried repeatedly that I was going to die. My partner sat with his face buried in his hands. I felt timeless and adrift, connected to a long line of women through history for whom death in childbirth was a real threat. I begged the surgeon not to cut me. I became hysterical, then unnervingly calm. I could feel the shape of the instruments before they touched my skin, feel the surface of the bed and the hard floor beneath it, my own bones under my useless skin. I imagined I could feel every one of the baby's fingers and toes inside me, slippery with blood. My body was a vehicle for my child and yet I was becoming skinless, turning into the room. I was a climber, briefly and unexpectedly at one with the gathering storm, the threat of avalanche, the last hour of daylight, the escape routes closing ahead like doors in a long, white corridor.

I remembered the feeling of falling from a rock face in Derbyshire, that weightless rush before the rope was stopped by my gear, the lurch and hold. I was tumbling through space, then I was caught. And the ghost that I hallucinated there with me, connected to the rope, was my ex helping me up Ama Dablam, the jewelled mother mountain. Even in my altered state, I felt a tightening of embarrassment, then a hot flush of guilt. It seemed an involuntary betrayal. On the cusp of birth I had one foot in my old life, the imagined freedom of climbing with someone else. How could I ever tell my partner? It's said that when they reach the transitional stage in labour – the point where the body prepares to push – women often try to leave the room, talk about going home. They experience the urge to run away. Midwives know this as a sign that the birth is actually progressing well and the baby is close. I was on the threshold of my life as a mother and I was clambering impatiently out of my own body, looking for vertical edges, trying to claw my way back towards the sky, the way I learned to when I discovered rock climbing.

In the decade after we first met, Andrew and I climbed all over the world: in Scotland and in Sheffield, in Europe and in Canada, parched places, frozen places, slabs and glaciers and scree slopes and hidden ledges where I thought I knew exhaustion, the metallic taste and sink of it. Sometimes we were a couple and sometimes we were not. Sometimes we climbed as friends. Sometimes we climbed with others. But I always came back to our ropes and our plans and our shared silences. There was a constancy to our climbing. He was always calm and measured, assessing the shape of each route, touching the rock patiently. We practised ice-axe arrests below Ben Nevis in winter, hurling ourselves at the snow, hanging on for dear life. We ran for two days through the Munros in high summer, carrying our camping gear on our backs, plunging through bog and heather. I didn't trust my own navigational instincts, deferred to his knowledge of the land, his capacity to read a map and understand that the 2D representation of place was a landscape in itself, terrain that had to be respected. I was too distracted by the differences, amazed by the immediate colours of heather, the changing things the map couldn't hold. I made impulsive judgements while he was always so much more reliable than me.

In some ways, the decision to become a mother had felt like that: impulsive, instinctive, irrational. It came from somewhere beyond me and inside me at the same time. I was swimming in a cold loch on New Year's Day 2017, a small and sunlit body of water somewhere between Gairloch and Ullapool, Scotland's remote northwest coast. Later, I learned it was called Tollaidh, meaning 'place of the holes'. The landscape seemed pitted all around me, scooped-out beaches, hollows of moss, abandoned barns. It was a place I'd come to empty my head. On the drive north earlier that week, I'd felt something spreading under my skin. Thinking of my mother and my grandmother and my dead great-grandmother as I accelerated away from my childhood home, from Christmas and my tiny teenage bedroom, was a welling, pooling sensation. I pulled into a lay-by, switched off the engine of my car and wept. The tears surprised me. They were selfish tears, for the child I would never be again, for deaths that had not yet happened, for my own unaccountable loneliness, a life structured around pleasing myself. I was driving to Scotland to see out the old year on my own in a tiny cottage. The village I'd chosen – Laide – was storm-swept and rattled when I arrived. Nights in the cottage were long, echoing and spooky. I cooked pasta and drank neat whisky, smoked under the cold stars. I kept the light on when I slept. On New Year's Eve, Andrew came to visit me on his way to see his family near Glasgow. I had planned to be alone, but I almost wept again with relief when he hugged me, asked nothing of me. We chased the old year out with wine. In the morning, the first day of January, we wanted to swim. We needed to be immersed.

Andrew was always somewhere in front of me. I swam out further than I should have and, when I turned around, had the sensation of hardly being able to move with the cold. Every stroke was an effort. Andrew was on the shoreline, drying himself. His pale skin was a shock against the gold of the winter grass and the pewter sky. Desire and tenderness mingled. One was rain and the other sky, one cut through the other, one was visible, both were there. I wanted something to swim in me. I wanted to hold something the way the lake held me. To be a vessel and an element, known and unknown. I wanted to be a mother. The realisation made me feel light-headed, almost nauseous. C*ould we have a child?* I wanted to keep swimming, to lose the sensation in all my limbs, to numb myself completely. Andrew was photographing the winter light over Slioch, framed in his own world. I hauled myself from the water, seal-slick, and pretended that nothing had changed. I struggled out of my wetsuit in the back of Andrew's car, making a pantomime of it. We drove to Gairloch and drank hot chocolate in a cafe where Shania Twain blasted from the speakers and the walls were lined with pictures of mountains. I was giddy with the cold. I sang and danced. *Man, I feel like a woman.*

That moment is frozen, water under the surface of a loch. It is still, full of promise, holding ache and fear and excitement. I hadn't met the father of my child then. That all came later, happened quickly, the year gathering speed around me. There is a vertigo to my memory of it. By March 2018, I had a different life. Andrew and I spoke less often. I had all but abandoned climbing and I knew I was expecting a baby. During my pregnancy, I spent a lot of time imagining what it would be like to give birth, as if visualising my fears would take away some of their potency. I was perhaps most afraid of losing control, of my body not feeling like my own. For months, I tried to imagine the sensation. When it came to it, in the birthing suite, I felt as if my body was turning itself inside out. With every push, I wanted to hold myself back. I was terrified of losing my bones, my muscles and all my slick internal organs. I gripped the side of the chair, scrabbling for something to hold on to, something to anchor me.

I was back on the Stawamus Chief in Squamish, British Columbia, balancing on granite, trusting my feet to friction and good luck. The sun was a hot knife on my neck. Andrew and I climbed a multi-pitch route called Diedre which snaked up following fissures and cracks in the rock. I had never moved on granite before. It seemed featureless and intimidating, a silver page in an unwritten book. Below, there were pine trees and parking lots, parched streets and scrubland. It became possible to stand on nothing, the rubber soles of my shoes cleaving to the rock. But to make the move and gain height, I'd have to let go for a millisecond, trust the sheerness I was standing on, the smooth appearance of the granite. I looked down and the earth shelved away from me. I looked up and the sky was powder blue, languid, a calm sea. To my left and right the rock was endless. I rocked over onto my right foot, let it take all of my weight, then I reached upwards in one fluid movement. It was an instant of uncertainty. Then I was safe and the rope was tightening again, I was held from above. I moved quickly, whistling and sweating, feeling the prickle of my raw shoulders and the pinch of my toes in my boots. The route became a dance with the moves already mapped out for us. At the top, we were light and clear-headed, giggling with pride. We couldn't get enough of climbing that day. Once we'd scrambled down to the base of the route, we hauled ourselves up a crack called Seasoned in the Sun, jamming our hands and toes into the gap, torquing our bodies. Every movement was an effort, felt in our lungs and battered fingertips. When we were spent, we ambled back into Squamish and drank lager so cold it beaded the glass, looking back at where we'd just been, the height and smoothness suddenly incomprehensible to us.

*

What we seek in climbing, I think, is a passionate dance with control. When you climb a rock face or a mountain, you expose yourself to risks that come from somewhere beyond you. The gear you've placed might fail, an avalanche might sweep you from the face, a storm might swell from nowhere, a lump of rock might sheer off beneath your hands. And yet you can minimise the threats you face with experience, good judgement and humility. You can make wise gear placements, plan carefully, scrutinise the conditions. Climbing gives you the illusion of being in control, just for a while, the tantalising sense of being able to stay one move ahead of death. It is an experiment in fear. It is somehow far less overwhelming than everyday life. The truth is, no matter how talented you are, how prudent, how skilled, each climb is a gamble. For most people who love mountains, a time in life comes when the roll call of the dead begins to outnumber the roll call of the living. Death is abstract, until it isn't. Mountaineering is a dangerous and uncertain game. It claims the strongest, fittest and sharpest among us. Yet the illusion of control persists. It has to, or we wouldn't do it. In the hospital, I found myself wondering if birth offers the same illusion. I remembered the books and breathing exercises and hypnobirthing CDs, the meditation, the woman who told me I should take my mind to a quiet place, the shadows under the canopy of a tree. When I entered the water of the birthing pool, I let all those ideas go, abandoned myself to the agonised moment, let it squeeze the breath out of me. There were no shaded trees. I was out of control. Beyond it. My mind was useless to me. My body was forging ahead, carrying me through the night, delivering my son. There was no other imperative.

In 1994, British climber, mother and athlete Alison Hargreaves was at the Banff Mountain Film and Book Festival in Canada, participating in a special international panel on women and adventure. She had recently returned from Nepal where she had made an unsuccessful attempt on Everest, accompanied by her husband and two children as far as base camp. Her unusual decision to take her daughter and son with her had attracted a huge amount of media interest. At the Banff festival event, Alison was the only person on the panel who had continued to climb after becoming a mother. The moderator opened the discussion by saying how astonished she was to learn that Hargreaves 'did the climbing she did with two young children', echoing the criticisms already levelled at her in the press. Another panellist, the American mountaineer Arlene Blum, revealed that she'd had her daughter only after she had already achieved most of her major climbing goals. Objective danger was no longer of any interest to her. Alison was strident in her reply:

> As far as I'm concerned, 99 per cent of objective dangers you can be in control of. If a serac falls on you . . . generally it was your decision to be there. If you're on a glacier when it's dangerous, then you were wrong [to be there]

Alison's life was built around her pull to mountains, and it was sustained by faith: the self-belief she was able to maintain in some of the world's most dangerous environments. Born in Belper, Derbyshire, her early climbs around the UK filled her with joy, abseiling down ropes into the unknown, counting the stars above her on Scottish winter nights. Climbing offered control and freedom all at once. Her best friend, Bev, was a climber too and they went on adventures together, two girls in oversized down jackets, finding their way in a male-dominated world. When Alison was still a teenager, she left home and moved in with the owner of the outdoor shop where she worked, Jim Ballard, an older divorcee. Though bright and successful enough at school, she committed herself to a lifestyle that would allow her to climb as much as possible, making rock routes and mountains the centre of her life. In time, she developed an international reputation, climbing the great north faces of the Alps alone and in a single season, summiting the highest mountain in the world without supplementary oxygen.

Her need to climb was undiminished when she became a mother in 1988. She even scaled the north face of the Eiger while she was six months pregnant with her son, Tom. Until I had my own son, this seemed abstract. I read about her achievement and thought her daring, strong. But when I was pregnant, my own sense of risk changed. Adventure suddenly felt like indulgence. I panted my way up Munros in my second trimester and walked furtively, guiltily, fearing every trip and stumble. I covered my bump with loose waterproof jackets. I imagined the censure of every hiker I passed. Descending Snowdon at six months pregnant, I slipped on wet stones on the Miners' Track and landed heavily on my back. For weeks, the face in the mirror reproached me. Alison was not afraid of judgement, or if she was, she didn't acknowledge it. When anyone challenged her decisions, she calmly repeated the same story. Climbing wasn't about taking risks, it was about controlling them. If you died, it was because of carelessness. She was widely regarded as a safe, competent and strong climber, bold but wise, plucky but careful.

Yet that isn't the only image of Alison that has endured. In 1995, shortly after her success on Everest, Alison went to Pakistan to attempt K2, 'the savage mountain'. It was a trip she would never return from. She was 33 years old, the same age I was when I birthed my child, when I made my melodramatic pronouncements about death in the Royal Hospital. But after the forceps and the medieval-looking instruments, after the blood loss and fear, I lay beached on my bed in the ward with my son in my arms. When they pulled him out and placed him on me, he seemed to rear up, impossibly strong, impossibly determined. I held him to my chest. Because I did not know what else to do, because the surgeon was stitching me after my episiotomy and the local anaesthetic was wearing off and I was agonised, I just patted him, whispered, 'It's OK,' over and over again. I said his name: Alfie. I had lost a litre and a half of blood, I felt drained and lifeless. But I was holding a bundle of fierce life, bunched energy, pure instinct. My world had never been more animated. I felt the mix of peace and vertigo that comes at the top of a hard climb.

My first introduction to mountaineering was through the literary canon of adventure writing, classic books by great men. When I began to read about female climbers – Lynn Hill and Julie Tullis, Catherine Destivelle and Dorothy Pilley – I was filled with admiration and wonder, but they seemed like a different species. Reading about them from my box room in a house outside Chesterfield with pylons humming outside and the noise of open casting from Arkwright Town felt abstract. But when I read about Alison Hargreaves in the ground-breaking biography Ed Douglas and David Rose published in 1999, everything changed, risk became tangible. To a hungry, lost teenager, Alison was a woman of tireless passion, unpredictable and wild. She was made of heather and dark stone, moss and well dressings, big skies and rough edges. She was a Derbyshire girl like me, brought up in a bookish household. She wrote a diary where she affected a mannered persona, just like my teenage journal, pretending to be someone else. She daydreamed, lived for moments of escape. She was happiest running for hours over the moors, running until the distance seemed unimportant and she was alone with the curlews and grouse and deer and rain. She was animated, ambitious, often contradictory. She was drawn to older men, to the world of experience and certainty and promise. I didn't know the thrill of elite climbing, of being skilled like her, of standing on the roof of the world. But I recognised her. Even her face – round and lively, framed by dark hair – seemed comforting. I knew what it was to run until you felt you might catch fire, take off with no destination. I knew what it was to love unwisely, feel intensely, escape from a small town into silence and height. And I have come to know what it is to be a mother, to hold a screaming newborn child in your arms and realise that you have climbed high, higher than you thought possible, realise that there is no way down from here.

/\ APPROACH

Great Langdale is a vase of rain. It's early autumn and the ground is soggy, burnished, tired of the summer's heat. Twigs underfoot, brown leaves tipped with gold, a mulch of them. You squint up at the sky and frown, your face dampened. Drizzle hangs in the air, almost glittering. September is glamorous here, the Langdale Pikes in their veil of sky, the Old Dungeon Ghyll Hotel with its windows already lit, diamonds of water in the long grass. You shoulder your rucksack onto your back, blue rope tucked neatly under the straps, and set off from the car park, taking the path behind the pub, crossing the stream. Wet stones, an ancient, creaking gate.

She follows. When you look back at her, your face is the daytime moon, known and surprising. You are tall, with your father's shoulders. Your mouth is a bud, your hair fawn-coloured and thick. You have blue eyes and a small nose, a mole on your temple. Your stubble is sand. There is a single vein always half visible in your neck, pumping the good blood around your body, throbbing with life. You are never completely still. When you smile, you are handsome. You're wearing your favourite jacket, rust-orange, a wind-blown leaf. You are heavy-footed. The track accepts your stride.

The path is steep. Rain lessening now, a crow arcing overhead. The sky is all cloud. Between boulders, bracken has been sharpened by damp, its scent cloying. Herdwick sheep amble up the fellside, grazing, bleating. There is an empty stone shelter on the track. The path leads away from it, up towards the crag.

At the foot of the buttress, near a skinny fence, you stop and put down your bag. Your chest rises and falls – you're sweating slightly with effort. You turn round to take in the valley, the pewter of the river, the comforting shape of the pub, the silent mountains. Then you attend to your rucksack, opening the clasps, releasing the drawstring, taking out your things one by one and setting them on the ground: the cams and nuts and belay device, the slings and hexes.

You step your feet into your harness and pull it up over your jeans, adjusting the leg loops and the waist. Snug. You pick up a blue quickdraw and clip it to the back of the harness, then another. The sound as it snaps shut is satisfying. You take the largest cam, the purple size 4, and clip that. Smaller cams next, the shiny nubs of them. The lucky purple cam, the one that seems to fit anywhere. You clip on nuts, some new, some second-hand and battered, scratched with wear. You loop a sling around your chest and clip two karabiners to it. The others go on your harness, next to your belay device. When you move, you jangle.

The blue rope is the first to be untied. It always goes on the left-hand side. Up close, it isn't pure blue at all, but flecked with purple and yellow. Next, the yellow. It goes on the right. You pay it out, making sure there are no tangles or knots. Then you attach both to your harness with a figure of eight, finished with a stopper knot. You slip on your helmet. You won't consider the route until your shoes are on, their Velcro fastened, rubber pinching at your toes. Then you can look at the rock face to face, an equal, taller than you and more solid, morose with weather. There's a breeze and the rock is drying quickly, its colours lightening. You whistle under your breath. You were named after a man who was always whistling, always humming, who carried tunes with him wherever he went, always kept a cigarette hanging from his lip. An ancestor you never met.

Your body interrupts the season, bright and quick. There is brief light on the crag, lemony sun. For a second, everything is spotlit, golden. You have everything you need. You cough nervously, clear your throat. Then you murmur, 'Climbing.'

GHOST TWIN

2021

It's early January, anaemic light, the trees in the garden still quivering from birds that have left them, robins and slim jays, flecked with near-electric blue. The new year is beginning, lifting its weary bones from the sleeping ground and shaking off the earth. The lawn is veined with frost. All last night, foxes sounded their bleak desires across my street, guttural sounds from bodies made efficient by cold. I lay awake, imagining them filling the gaps of early morning with their movements, burrowing under sheds and hedges, complicating the fretwork of shadows on Brincliffe Edge, running up the hillside towards moorland, framed and caught briefly by the light of the moon. They were so loud it seemed they were reclaiming the city as their own, making it lithe again. Their cries boomed and echoed.

I stood at the window at 2am and 3am, looking at the rain-glittered tarmac, the empty street. They were heard and not seen. I wanted to answer them. The first night of the first day of the new year: a time for beginnings, for change, for burning old resentments and failures by candlelight and forging resolutions with your breath and blood. I ended the old year with a swim in the river at Chatsworth, struggling against a freezing current that wanted to carry me away. Afterwards, I hung my wetsuit up like a skin I no longer needed. Slumped, inadequate body. Begin. Begin again. Run feral with the night creatures, bin-raiders and dawn-dodgers. But I do not know how to start again. In the years since my son was born, I have struggled to find the edges of myself, failed to make time to write, to run, to be solitary and unencumbered. I have forgotten myself. Writing requires me to remember. And memory is sharp, painful, difficult, honed like the blade of an ice axe.

Instead of writing, my first instinct is to find the place where gritstone begins, where it first shows itself, pushing up through the landscape west of the city. It is freezing now, the sky has been pregnant with snow for days, frost touching the roads with its liquid, slippery promise. I scrape the ice from my car windows with the only flat object I can find, a part of a wooden car my two-year-old son likes to take apart and build again. I crawl down our road, houses still quiet, pavements unwalked, and begin a journey I've made countless times before, skirting the woods and then climbing slowly up Ringinglow Road, past the large detached houses and the school where my stepdaughter goes, past the farms and the brick facade of the Norfolk Arms, the plantation and the small roads that lead back down to Sheffield and the Mayfield Valley.

With the plantation behind me, the verges are a shock of white, terrified by snow, deep with promise. The cloud is low over the moors, a coin-perfect sun struggling to rise. There are no other cars save for one abandoned in a lay-by, sealed with frost. Soon, it is too dangerous to drive on. I have entered a lunar landscape, everything bleached and muffled, the rocks hidden from view. My world becomes immediate. My car skids and I remind myself to steer into the movement, use gears instead of brakes. Eventually, I come to a halt. I am in a parking-area-cum-ice-rink. I switch off the engine. I clamber out and begin to run. For miles, my breath makes a trail that my body follows. My legs tingle with cold until they spark. The whole of the Great Ridge is somewhere before me, the steep world. At home, my son will just be stirring now, singing to himself in his cot. My husband will turn over in his sleep, groggy from the night. I don't have much time. I make firm prints in the snow. This is the first part of writing. This is how I begin to speak.

When I try to articulate my relationship with the mountaineer Alison Hargreaves, I always find myself stopped by guilt. The problem is in the word *relationship*, for ours is entirely one-sided, built on imagined conversations, grafted text, feverish dreams. This is a non-consensual partnership. Only one of us is alive, only one of us can defend themselves, speak their desires. What is Alison to me? A name. A biography. A clipped voice on old recordings. An image from the afterlife, frozen by the camera, leaning into steepness and snow. What gives me the right to weave her story into my own, narrate the life and death of someone I never climbed with, never even met? What do I see in her black-and-white photograph, her slight body and wide smile?

If I go to look for her, she is nowhere. At Stanage and Black Rocks, her fingers left no visible imprint on the gritstone. When I walk the hemmed streets of her Belper childhood, I find no ghosts, only trimmed houses, neat lawns and familiar shops, a park with manicured hedges. But I imagine her everywhere, breathing steadily in my ear, a shape disappearing into mist on the summit plateau of Kinder Scout, vanishing behind the grotesque shapes of the Woolpacks, a clump of gritstone formations, squat and imposing. Whenever I climb or run or walk alone in bad weather, it's her I think of. Perhaps I should not ask what is she to me but what am I to her? Nothing. Less than nobody. I was never in her life and now that she's dead I never will be. And yet. There is something comforting in that transparency, in being unseen, being unknown. In chasing her ghost, I become a ghost in my own life. I give myself permission to pass through walls, slip underneath the surface of the ice, stare up at her from underwater, auditioning to be her wobbly reflection. For a writer, this is comforting, familiar territory. I like nothing better than to watch, to fill my notebook with eavesdroppings, to forget myself in the service of something intangible.

In the first image I ever saw of Alison Hargreaves, she is in her early 30s, wearing a dark green Sprayway jacket and a wide smile, hair tied back with a black headband, face angled towards the mountains that frame her as if she wants to tilt the flame of herself towards the Himalaya. Her cheeks are flushed by cold, her arms hang loosely by her sides, fingers curled as if they recently held something. I remember wondering what she might have had in her hands, how firmly her crampons were anchored in the snow, what she had in her pockets. In all her mountaineering photos, there is both something slight and something substantial about her.

Even as a teenager, I recognised something of myself in that sturdiness, that fragility. The physical paradox of her. I have pored over photos of her like a schoolgirl with a crush. Alison with a red rucksack and axes planted deep in ice. Alison emerging from her expedition tent, unsmiling or drinking from a metal cup at base camp. Alison on the cover of her own book, space and air above and below her. Alison carrying a child on each arm, turning to look at her son. But it is that first picture I always return to, her shining eyes and knowing expression, her refusal to look square at the camera, to stand straight. I think of it and I tilt towards her, reaching.

Most of all, I want to write to her. Or to her ghost. Can I admit that I prefer her company to the living, to the noise of family life that fills my days and makes them brim over? I grew up in hush, no siblings to fight or play with in a semi-detached house lost between one small town and another. Now, I live with my husband, our toddler, his teenage daughter and sometimes his adult son, Leo. We have a bold, inquisitive cat. Often there are boisterous dogs in the house, a Labrador–beagle cross and a cocker spaniel. Then there are Leo's friends and his girlfriend, Anjali. There is always loud music, drumming, footsteps racing up and down stairs, clattering pans, slamming doors, running water. It is glorious. But it is not my natural habitat. There is an exquisite loneliness in being an only child, an isolation I fear and guard in equal measure. The urge to run away and the urge to reach out to others. This, I fear, is what makes me a writer, someone who always feels like an observer in a crowd, an outsider in a group. For me, writing is an unstable bridge to the world, a way of keeping it close without letting it touch me.

Before I wrote books, I wrote stories in notebooks. Before I wrote stories, I wrote letters. Ever since I was ten, I've had pen pals. There was the older girl in Australia who I corresponded with when I was at primary school, thrilled by the navy-blue-and-white importance of the air mail stickers, imagining my letters handled reverently in the post office. I often imagined her too, deciding she had sun-bleached hair and a permanent tan, teeth like boulders when she smiled. There was Zoe from Whitehaven, Cumbria, whose handwriting lurched across the page. She described the ex-industrial coastline of the North West to me and I tried to make the pylons keeping vigil behind my house interesting, told her about the mystery farm down Oaks Lane where a tethered dog barked itself hoarse and rabbits skittered into furrows but no human was ever seen. I wrote to imaginary friends too, or spoke to absent audiences: I spent hours recording my own radio shows at night with the lights dimmed, speaking into an old tape recorder. Clunks and whirrs when I made a mistake and wanted to record over it. Songs tinnily reproduced from the radio. Seal's 'Kiss from a Rose'.

I think my childhood taught me to understand and crave these silent presences, the need to speak to someone who will not answer back, who walks one step behind or just in front, enticingly out of reach, their prints in the snow covered when you look down. Blank snow. Blank page before the pen ruins it. Perhaps only children are particularly alert to these ghosts. When I was old enough to hear it, my mother told me that when she was pregnant with me an ultrasound scan seemed to briefly show two heartbeats and the doctors thought she was having twins. My parents had given up on conceiving altogether at the point when I began to grow. One child had seemed unlikely, let alone two. In the end, there was only one of me. There is no evidence for my vanishing twin. Perhaps it was an anomaly, a mistake, a ghost in the machine. There is no proof. Just a lingering feeling of incompleteness, expressed when I was young as short-lived desire for a sibling I could never have. It seems strange to me now that I was so adamant: I feel solitary by nature, keeping the world at arm's length while I watch and take notes. I think of Louis MacNeice and his poem 'Snow': 'There is more than glass between the snow and the huge roses.' I have always loved that line. Things that seem close are distant. Seeing the outside is not the same as reaching it.

I believe in ghosts. Or at least I do not disbelieve in them. I have a prurient interest in anecdotes that confirm the Third Man factor, the idea that explorers in turmoil are often joined by an 'other' who watches over them. Whenever I climb solo, I'm most aware of the sensation of being watched. It isn't a particularly troubling or sinister feeling, just the certainty of another presence. Once, climbing easy routes on Stanage Edge, the afternoon so storm-swept there was no one else around, I felt the prickling intensity of someone else's gaze. When I scrambled down from the gritstone lip, the crag was still deserted. A single hawk was hovering above me, quivering a circle in the air. Its body appraised mine. In *Explorers of the Infinite*, a study of mountains and the supernatural, Maria Coffey – the partner of mountaineer Joe Tasker who disappeared along with Pete Boardman on Everest in 1982 – argues that the survival of extreme adventurers depends on a kind of hypervigilance, heightened awareness of their surroundings. Climbers are constantly monitoring their sensory world – the texture of rock under their fingers, how their crampons bite into the ice and hold, subtle shifts in weather. They're like rabbits, twitching their noses, assessing, testing the air. Their lives depend upon this process, this pattern-finding. It's what most of us call intuition, knowing something instinctively. Joe Tasker would have been no stranger to presence, to mystery – born in a religious family, he had trained as a Catholic priest before becoming a climber. Yet his instincts could not save him. The body of Pete Boardman was found in 1992, resting in a sitting position just past a pinnacle on the middle North-East Ridge of Everest, but the body of Tasker is still missing, the only trace of him a clutch of his climbing equipment, found between the pinnacles. Belongings.

Maria has spent half her lifetime making sense of Joe's death, exploring the spiritual aspects of climbing, wondering whether becoming highly attuned to nature leads to mountaineers opening channels to hidden powers, realms of experience that we call mystical and paranormal. Members of early expeditions hallucinated strange colours, unfamiliar sounds. On the famous 1924 Everest attempt, the trip on which George Mallory and Sandy Irvine disappeared, Howard Somervell heard human voices warning his party to go 'thus far and no further'. Somervell and his climbing partner had reached 28,128 feet on Everest's North Face without using artificial oxygen, a monumental effort. Eating and drinking would have been difficult, the effects of oxygen deprivation inducing a state where doggedly putting one foot in front of another was the only thing he was able to focus on. Many climbers at altitude are said to be gripped by 'summit fever', the compulsion to reach the top of the mountain at any cost, but Somervell felt warned from continuing by a voice from beyond him. His friends Mallory and Irvine would never return from their summit bid.

Nobody can be sure if these ghostly sightings, these sensed presences, are the effects of extreme altitude, oxygen deprivation, exhaustion, or something less neat, less knowable, more mysterious. When I imagine the mountain ghosts, I think of the Brocken spectre I saw with my father one Boxing Day in Litton in the White Peak. Snow clung to the limestone and, above it, there was a misty figure, haloed with a rainbow of light, all the colours of the landscape warped and blooming around it, as if its outline had punched through sky and opened another world. There was a rational explanation. It was only my magnified shadow, cast on clouds opposite the sun's direction, but I wept at it and as we walked on I felt myself followed. There was strange comfort in that. I often go to the hills alone because I'm restless around other people, find myself distant in a crowd. But sometimes my loneliness follows me and I cannot walk it off. I crave the companionship of things that will not answer back, streams that vanish underground, the prints of small animals, lichen touched by water.

Sleeping on a coffin-sized rock in Tilberthwaite Quarry when I was in my 20s and loved climbing well past dusk, I dreamed a huge lurcher was running loops around me, a moving patch of night, fluid in his baggy skin, nose to the ground. In Greenland in 2016, I became preoccupied with the polar bears we had not seen. We spent hours hauling rocks and positioning wires around our camp to deter bears from coming too close, learned how to trigger flares to startle them should they be curious or hungry enough to stray near supplies they could smell 20 miles away. We only saw the bears through the traces they left: crossing a huge glacier, we encountered what looked like a rusty tangle of wire, stark among the white. Perhaps it was the guts of a seal, possibly dropped from the jaws of a bear who had crossed the glacier before us, a polar bear highway. On our last night at camp, I could not sleep, agitated by the sounds of restless birds outside who seemed to be startled by something, flocking as one. I was convinced that there was a bear somewhere within calling distance, still and regal, nose testing the air. When we woke in the morning, Matt – a guide with decades of experience in Greenland – had sensed the same thing.

The poet John Burnside shares my preoccupation with ghost twins, with absent companions. I never tire of his poem 'The Good Neighbour', its opening image of an 'unknown' man on the same street as the narrator, living 'behind a maze of apple trees and stars', his life played out in parallel:

> He listens for the bird lines in the clouds
> and, like that ghost companion in the old
> explorers' tales, that phantom in the sleet,
> fifth in a party of four, he's not quite there
> but not quite inexistent, nonetheless.

Is Alison Hargreaves my own 'good neighbour', my own conjured presence? Is it her I wait for at the window at 2am and 3 and 4?

*

When I re-read *Regions of the Heart*, Alison's biography, as an adult, I was living back on the street where I grew up. This was part comfort, part defeat: I was studying for a PhD at the University of Sheffield and my parents were helping to take care of my dogs, a pair of affectionate, needy whippets. I had come home, almost. Behind my terraced house was the wreckage of the working men's club I drank in as a teenager, dismembered fruit machines and the remnants of optics. Behind that, the power station, the rain-slicked lanes that snaked towards Hasland, farms with scraggy horses tethered by the fences, collies guarding dank yards. Everything was on the verge of being beautiful, especially in winter when it snowed. There were tracks through the fields I'd never noticed as a kid, hidden fields with Traveller caravans moored in them. But there was dog shit and kids smoking on the wall outside my front room, cradling tinnies from the shop next door. I kept my curtains drawn. All my furniture was salvaged from relatives, my cupboards stuffed with ancient cutlery. I had an under-stairs storage cubbyhole where I crammed all the things the previous tenants had left behind, false flowers and porn DVDs with topless girls in roller skates and knee socks on the covers. All night, my neighbours screamed at each other. The back of the house had a makeshift roof and the weather poked its face through, found me in my dressing gown on the off-pink sofa, imagining myself into Alison's early life in Belper. I read *Regions of the Heart* that second time in one sitting. And I wept at her loss, at her frustrated ambitions, the motherless children she left behind.

After I finished it, I wrote sheafs of poems addressed to Alison, much like the letters I sent to distant pen pals when I was a child, those cheerful girls I had never met. I began with scrawled lines, scribbled justifications:

> I write to you because your imprint's everywhere
> across the landscape's leaned-on page . . .

That is how the Peak District National Park seems to me: jammed between Sheffield and Manchester, it is populous, thronging, bearing the marks of countless people passing. On a busy day, Stanage is like a sheaf from someone's journal, a record of activity. Alison's journal. I loved the quoted extracts from her diaries, the mannered optimism of them. I admired the detail with which she catalogued familiar routes and the brevity given to almost everything else, how she barely mentioned her first kiss. On Tuesday nights, I'd drive out to Wharncliffe or Baslow Edge or Curbar and climb until it was dark with friends of my dad who remembered Alison, had met her or seen her. One evening, I led Sunset Slab at Froggatt with Alison's description of it echoing in my head. I climbed better than I ever had before and had virtually no memory of it afterwards, as if I had borrowed her body, her fluency, her movements. In the pub later, nursing my half of pale beer, I asked questions quietly, almost furtively. What gave me the right to take such an interest in her life? When she died, I was just ten years old.

It's easy to imagine the lives we might have lived. Why else do men crowd around the TV in my local every Sunday, shouting abuse or praise at football players they feel connected to? These players in numbered shirts are known unknowns. I must acknowledge the childish, hopeful part of me that believes that, in different circumstances, I could have forged my identity around mountains in the way Alison did. This is part arrogance, part extrapolation. Even writing it down feels shameful. Her ambition, her background and her insecurities are all familiar to me. I share her utter joy in mountains and

their redemptive power. I have unusual reserves of fitness, lung capacity which would make me suited to expeditions in high mountains, the stamina they sap from the body. I'm a mediocre rock climber, but perhaps I would have been a skilled mountaineer if I had the drive and effort. These are big ifs. I made different choices. I have pursued writing with the same dogged persistence that Alison pursued climbing, keeping something secret in my body, something that can never really be shared by others. It's often said that to write well, poets have to keep a sliver of ice in their heart. Mountain ice. I imagine Alison chipping at a slanted piece of ice with her axes, a blueish shard that she cupped in the palm of her hand, a corner of the mountain that began to melt even as she touched it. I imagine it passing through the thick layers of her waterproofs and down, base layers and skin, muscles and sinew, the barred wings of her ribcage. I imagine it finding a home somewhere scant between blood and bone. There are places we must protect from the intrusion of others.

Now, as a mother, I often imagine that family has tamed me, that it prevents me from running free in the mountains and travelling unencumbered in the way I used to. I know this is naive. Besides, I have tamed myself. Alison's example shows that, with enough resilience, with enough care, mothers can keep their wildness. I am something like the kitten we adopted from a local rescue centre when Alfie was old enough to be entertained by pets. When she arrived, she was furtive and striking, amber eyes and markings that seemed part Bengal. She slunk low to the ground, pounced on our feet, clambered her way up the chimney, sat in the sink swiping at droplets of water from the tap. We talked excitedly about what a good hunter she would be when she was finally allowed outside. Daring, quick to catch. After weeks of careful supervision, we opened the door to let her explore her new kingdom, the rockery and the gravel, the reeds guarding the pond, the eucalyptus tree and the herb beds. As soon as she felt the draught on her whiskers, she froze. She glanced at me, at the expanse outside, at the room that contained her. Then she ran towards the sofa. This happened seven or eight times before she ventured out. I can't help feeling that I've settled into life as a house cat, that I am shunning the open door. Nobody to blame but myself.

*

I have always been a cautious climber, tentative. At my strongest, my boldest, I used to try routes at the limit of my ability, but I'd usually find ones that had an escape route nearby, the potential for detouring and cheating. This is not always a wise strategy. At Rivelin, a crag on the outskirts of Sheffield nestled among trees, I once led a route called Better Late Than Never. It was a gently angled slab with little in the way of protection, little in the way of holds. Like many gritstone slabs, it was a series of committing moves with a break in the middle. It was a clammy day and my hands were sweating too much for the tiny holds, known as crimps. I danced my way up to the first break and faced an imposing section of blank rock. There was a small crack to my left which seemed like it might offer more purchase. 'Keep right,' my climbing partner Harry yelled up to me. 'Use friction.' Sometimes, knowing what you need to do does not increase your capacity to do it. I mimed moving my hands up, tested my rock shoes against the grit, afraid to put weight on them. I took heavy breaths, started to move three or four times only to backtrack. So much of climbing is like testing cold water. At the last moment, my nerve failed and I groped for safety to my left. In a second, my body was rippling away from the air, pressing its weight towards the ground. I stopped perilously close to Harry. Undeterred, I tried again. A bird of prey circled ominously overhead. The day seemed to pivot around the slab, kaleidoscopic. Again I moved. Again I flailed. Again I fell. Eventually, we packed up our gear and moved on. I had fallen because I didn't trust myself. I identify so much with Alison Hargreaves because I can imagine making the decisions she made. Deep down, I also doubt I'd have the nerve to execute them.

Since I gave birth to my son, I've found wildness in books. When I read, I feel as if I am receiving letters from a world I have forgotten, that mountains are still speaking to me, posting their messages through my suburban letterbox. In books, I can follow trails of my own longing, flanked by trees more vivid than any I've ever seen. The more grounded I feel, the more my body softens with motherhood, the more I seek images of freedom and peril. In the early months of Alfie's life, I read voraciously about bears, totems of mountain environments, survivors of a lost era. I sketched their shapes with my hands as if I could summon them, gnarled humps and glossy noses, wide paws with hard, black pads. I became obsessed with the habits of grizzlies, the hunger of sows. Bears that come from ranges and wilderness barely changed since the last ice age, who burrow into the foundations of mountains and winter there, birthing their blind, palm-sized cubs in the dark and letting them suckle greedily. Bears who emerge with the dawning warmth of spring, lumbering from their caves, descending across ridges and avalanche chutes, skirting houses and roads, unseen and unheard. Winter thins them, hunger drives them, the desperate need to pad the hollows beneath their shaggy fur with fat supplies, fodder for their next hibernation.

They are resourceful, ingenious, near-omnivorous, salvaging all that can be chewed, devouring the hidden nut stores of squirrels, uncovering cutworm moths and gleaming insects from behind boulders. They graze like cows and have snouts like dogs, impossibly sharp canine teeth. Their sense of smell is keener than a bloodhound's. They can follow a ribbon of scent for miles, propelled by need, made efficient by their intimacy with the cold, their knowledge of the dark, lean months. Active after dusk, they become moving patches of darkness, stalking the dreams of ranchers and their guard dogs, sensed but not seen. They are known as a stirring in the woods, noise in the bushes, given a wide berth. A sow with cubs is the most dangerous to encounter, feral with love. She will fight a boar to the death to protect her yearlings. Her paws can break the bones of an elk.

It is the menace and tenderness of bears that attracts me, I think, their complete otherness and their odd, aching familiarity, how human they seem when they stand on their hind legs, how human their cubs are. I have run unwisely in Canada at dawn alone, alert on the trails, knowing a grizzly could be close by. But I have only ever seen a bear once, a black bear cub, and even that encounter was tame. I was framed in the window of a Greyhound bus from Jasper to Vancouver, pale and listless, the only passenger awake at 5am, listening to bittersweet acoustic songs through my headphones. The bear was by the roadside, loping towards the shadows of trees, and almost stumbled as we passed. For a hundred miles, I thought of the arc of its back, its shambling gait. It was no threat. The only dangers on the highway were human. I didn't sleep because I was tense and edgy: years before, a passenger had been beheaded on a journey like this, throat slit by a man who had raised the machete almost casually, chosen his victim at random. I found comfort in the departing shape of the bear, its adolescent haunches and sleek fur.

In Sheffield, strobed by the TV, I yearn for bears and their habitat. Since he was tiny, my son's nickname has been Bear. He is solid, ambling, his compassion and rage know no bounds. His hands are large and his feet are great paws. He smells musky when he wakes up, burrows in the shallows behind trees, grubs in the ferns, catches things from ponds. With him, I am an animal, fierce and proud. I hold him to my belly at night and I nose him, sniff him, let him paw at me. But when I can't sleep, I long to take off into the night and flatten myself against moorland peat, roll in heather, taste the ground, alone and without him. I imagine creeping back in by morning, bringing him the smell of ferns, the taste of feathers, the roughness of gritstone, my eyes glittering with the small light the stars have granted me. I imagine that Alison felt like this. I imagine her sleepless and frayed, strung with desires she could barely name. I think of us as two sows in Montana, each guarding our patch of dark, our elk carcasses and rivers, wary and shy with our cubs, but staring at one another from separate outcrops, knowing the other's need, silent and wondering. In silence, she tells her story to me and I am thirsty, I drink it in great, cool gulps.

It is by chance that I pick up Francesca Wade's *Square Haunting* one fire-lit night, the biography of five women who lived in the same Bloomsbury neighbourhood – Mecklenburgh Square – at different periods in history. Some of them I know about: Virginia Woolf and her contemporaries. But when I reach the chapter on classics scholar Jane Ellen Harrison, I become attentive, absorbed. Harrison went up to Cambridge in 1874 to read Classics at Newnham, the place she would be most closely associated with for the rest of her life. She was the first woman in England to become an academic, in the fully professional sense – full-time, salaried, university researcher and lecturer. Those lectures were legendary, full-scale theatrical events that she toured around the country. She dressed for the occasion, famously in a shimmering beetle green, talking emphatically and always down to her audience, casting shadows over the hand-painted images of bearded serpents, using sound effects to captivate her audience. And through her exuberant, ardent writing on Ancient

Greece (thought heretical by some in the establishment) she changed the way we think about Greek scholarship for ever. But she was also a woman who worshipped bears. I stop short. Wade writes:

> Jane Harrison's scholarly interest in totemism was matched by her own deep love for bears of all forms . . . Frances Partridge, a student at Newnham, remembered Harrison's rooms being 'full of them – pictures of bears, wooden bears, silver bears. "I *love* bears," I hear her say in her deep voice.'

This fascination was no accident. In Ancient Greek culture, bears were revered – Aristotle identified man as unique in standing upright, but since this trait is shared by bears, they became sacred among the animals. What's more, they were associated with child-bearing and the female. I am pacing around the room with excitement as I read this. At the sanctuary of Artemis at Brauron, young girls would mark their transition to womanhood by dancing for the goddess in imitation of she-bears. Archaeological evidence includes hundreds of black-figure kraters that depict girls running foot-races and dancing, activities that were probably considered to be 'acting the she-bear'. And remains at the sanctuary site of Brauron included rows of small rooms built into a cave shelter, and date back to the 7th century BC. These have been suggested by scholars to mean that young girls would pretend to go into hibernation, like the she-bear, and emerge mature, as part of their worship to Artemis. When bears appear in Greek myths, their presence is often related to child-bearing. Two famous gods – Atalanta and Zeus – were recorded in antiquity to have been suckled by a she-bear. Other stories tell of mating with bears, children born half wild. They are commemorated in ancient artworks. Bears climbing rocks, regal and erect. Bears tormented by hunters. Solitary bears. For Jane Harrison, the semi-human aspects of the bear make it an ideal symbol, a figure on the margin between wildness/virginity and tameness/wifehood. Harrison never had children, feared she needed her work too badly to ever be a good mother. I feel a stab of guilt when I read this.

The fire is ebbing in the grate, flames reduced to embers. I stoke it with more wood, put on newspaper for the thrill of its momentary catch, favouring the short-term hit, the brief blaze. In the leap of the fire, I think I see young women with thorn-wild hair, bodies rising and falling, a hulking mimicry of she-bears. They rear on their hind legs and then crouch in the red dirt, knees scratched and tarnished. They dance themselves to oblivion, turning and bucking and crawling, bleeding and bruised, eyes lit copper and gold. They circle, keep their distance from one another. Behind them, parched mountains, shadowy and sparse. Above them, chimney-dark sky. I cannot see their faces. I only know that I am among them and that Alison Hargreaves is too, that we dance the same jerking rhythm, the same violent waltz, never touching one another, never getting close. The girl shapes rise and then crumple down to lumbering bears again, lumps of coal and wood.

I understand now. I know why we are there, together in the fire. I am fascinated by bears because I am not yet ready to become a woman, a mother, even though I have a child of my own. I am still grieving my own childhood, trying to outrun my new form, looking for places where I can be merely human, androgynous and wild. For Alison, that place was mountains. I am trying to follow her into the hills, into the bear-rich places of the world. But she is dead and I am lonely. My child is sleeping upstairs and in an hour to two hours he will need me to lift him from his cot, smooth his hair, rock him back and forth on my knees, reel off a list of the people who love him. *Dada loves you. Nana loves you. Baba loves you.* I think of how she-bears lie still and let their cubs go to them. *Sister loves you, brother loves you.* I always want to hold him in the curve of my knees, pressed against my belly. *Mama loves you. Most of all, Mama loves you.*

Sometimes he repeats a surreal incantation back to me. *Books love you. Nightlight loves you. Blanket loves you.* Those times, I hold him even tighter. I look to the cold sky, imagine I can find patterns in it, trace the constellation of Ursa Major, a delicate, silvery bear on all fours, head lifted lightly. This is what Alison would have seen from the Himalaya, so bright it must have seemed she could touch it. I go to bed in my safe, green-walled room. I dream of height.

/\/\ FIRST PITCH

Sometimes you forget you are climbing. It takes a few moves before you notice you've left the ground. Then you stop, breathe, think, *Here I am. Here.* Your steps are automatic, trailing the twin ropes behind you. You have chosen the most difficult start, the smoothest route up the first pitch of an easy buttress. Taking the path of most resistance. You have always been like this. As a toddler, you climbed the bannisters at the side of the stairs, swinging between them, feet slipping on painted white wood. You tried to climb up the silver slide in the playground, yelling angrily when your feet slipped, like walking on the surface of a mirror.

You glance down, step over the rope. The rock is starred with lichen, delicate and pale. You are repeating a well-loved sequence, following a pattern that others have traced before you: old men, kids, women scrambling in walking boots, the boy who lived in the pub and used to solo the buttress in his wellies after a shift at the bar. Easy. Just like that. A quick route and then home for tea. You can see their shapes, their outlines shimmying in front of you. You must match your body to theirs, make yourself light as a ghost, leave no record of your passage.

You are several metres off the ground and you haven't placed any gear yet. You stop, rummage through the cams on your harness, find a red size 2 and slot it under a niche. You tug at it to check the bite. Solid. You clip a quickdraw, then pull on the yellow rope, secure yourself. It's easy to forget the gear on a route like this, to be mesmerised by fluid movement. You're following a diagonal fissure in the rhyolite, keeping your feet on either side of it, bridging where you have to. The handholds are good, the footholds slightly precarious. They've been well polished by use and they're still damp. You move your left foot up onto something slippy, flinch, regain balance. Rhyolite sounds beautiful, insubstantial somehow. The word dissolves on your tongue.

Below, the valley echoes with farm machinery, cows lowing, the yaps of tethered dogs. Sometimes, there's the faint engine of a car, walkers setting off towards the Honister Pass. You imagine yourself dropped into the landscape like a coin in a well, ricocheting from crag to crag, spiralling down into scree and tarns and languid campsites, bouncing into oblivion. You think of the networks below ground, the strange rooms of earth and rock, how you'd drop through them, finding the dead centre of the earth. It would be silent there, silent and warm, like returning to the womb.

When you reach the first belay ledge, you realise you haven't placed any more gear. Below you, the route seems barely touched. It has already forgotten you. You coil the blue rope around a boulder, clip it, then fix yourself to a sling as well. You yell, 'Safe.' Then you haul the ropes in. Safe. Safe as a boulder. Safe as movement. Safe as the morning you pull around your shoulders for comfort, a thick shawl.

DESIRE PATHS

And one day, when I need
to tell myself something intelligent
about love,

I'll close my eyes
and recall this room and everything in it:
My body is estrangement.

– Li-Young Lee

2018

My life is made of lines. There is the line across the page that I'm making as I write this, casting out like a hopeful fisherman, praying the past will bite. There is the broken lifeline on my hand, the one a palm reader at a folk festival said meant premature death. There is the taut line made by a rope between two people climbing together, how it goes slack and tightens as one of them moves away from the other, heading towards the sun, calm and intent. Unspoiled line, perfected line. I have spent so many hours holding other people's ropes, staring at the intricate webbing of the blue nylon, giving slack and bracing for a fall. Some days, climbing feels entirely linear: the ascent of our bodies, the fissures and cracks and lines we look for in the rock and the horizontal strokes of gritstone edges. I love that simplicity of purpose. It comforts me. I love tracks and pathways, contour lines on a map, the sign for steepness. There is a line made by climbing and a line made by falling. There is the flawed line of my body. The parallel lines two bodies make. The line of someone walking into the distance. Someone else moving close. The line of want, the line of touch, of merging. Then there is the line of the pregnancy test, blue as the rope I climb with, slim and unforgettable.

I was in the mountains when I first knew I was pregnant. It was Easter, and my partner, Jess, had found a caravan perched on a hill a few miles outside Granada in Monachil, close to the Sierra Nevada mountains, the ridge that stretches across Andalucia in southern Spain. I remember sunlight and cold mornings, cats circling, a basket of almonds that we had to crack, foraging for the kernels inside the shells. We showered in the open air, navigated precarious roads overhung by rocks, ate salty tapas and drank strong coffee in the village square. Each day, we'd drive out to a peak we could climb.

Jess is not a mountain person, though he is intensely at home outdoors, more knowledgeable about trees and plants and creatures than I am, happiest outside. He loves ponds and caves, places of immersion. He comes from Lincolnshire, the flat, agricultural land that stretches towards the Fens, grew up on a farm. He's frequently gripped by vertigo. He can't walk along a thin ridge, the sheerness on either side terrifying to him. Through him, I have come to understand the fear of height, which is no failure of nerve: he is so much braver than me. Opposites attract. I love the things that we share but I admire our differences, our distinct heart-landscapes, the way he looks to the ground and I look to the sky. In Spain, we would sometimes walk a slope together and then I'd carry on to the top alone, leaving him with my rucksack, feeling light and unburdened. But I still felt connected to him, held in his sightline. There was a mountain called Boca de la Pesca, the mouth of the fish, and I revelled in its jagged peculiarity, waved to him from the summit. There's a photo of me on top of it: I look as if I'm perched on the head of a shark. Other times, we scrambled over ridges together, looked at the snowy flanks of the higher mountains beyond.

As I walked, I often felt strangely leaden, short of breath. One night, I felt a twinge in my abdomen, as if something small and sharp was travelling through me, a glass moth, a metal butterfly. When we went to walk round the Alhambra Palace, I was unbearably thirsty, downed two cans of Fanta from the vending machine. I felt unquenchable. One scorching afternoon, we took a path to a gorge following the rocks of a river and I sat down beside the banks and wept. I knew what was happening inside my womb. I felt the implantation, the first stirrings of new growth. It was hard to explain my blind certainty. Jess often deals in proof and rationalism. I deal in horoscopes, tarot cards, the lure of the mysterious, in lines that peter out and start again.

Geographers, urban planners and cartographers are preoccupied with desire lines, or desire paths, places where humans or animals have veered off the established trail and eroded their own way, forging a new route to a destination. This is a kind of trailblazing. Sometimes these lines are shortcuts, but sometimes they aren't. Their names form a litany: game trail, herd path, cow path, elephant path, goat track, pig track, use trail, bootleg trail. They are lines made deeper by use, signs of need, of want. The image of all these user-created paths, criss-crossing the earth, veering between the concrete, defying authority, has always appealed to me. Desire paths are telltale, the landscape scored with hope, the imperative to move. Perhaps they are inherently selfish: sometimes they cross protected land, stray into places that are fenced off.

For better or worse, I see my journey towards motherhood as a kind of desire path. My body had told me I wanted to be a mother and I had followed my instinct, made impulsive decisions, veered off the track I'd been shambling along all my life. And when I sat in the bathroom of our house in Sheffield, looking down at the white stick I was holding, the formation of that second, undeniable line, I was breathless, wondering how I'd got there, even though it was what we'd craved and wanted. I'd bought the test at the airport, desperate to know if my instincts were right. Now I trembled on the edge of the bath. I couldn't look directly at the test. I stared at the dust on the floor, how it gathered in corners, this room shabby with use, with the life we were building together.

I have always believed in what the body knows. In the ex-industrial flatlands of north-east Derbyshire where I grew up with a host of imaginary playmates, I had to trust in magic: fairies in the woods, dragons in the fields, enchanted gateposts on the way to school. In the playground, I was teased for my dreaminess and vague eccentricity. I used to make up commentaries in my head, pretend I was presenting my own television show. My imagination helped me survive. I also loved the quiet companionship of books. As I got older, the heroes in mountain literature replaced the imaginary friends I once pretended to play football with. I spent my days with Reinhold Messner and Walter Bonatti, Joe Simpson and Pete Boardman, men of ice and near-starvation, clinging on by the tips of axes, swinging above the void. My dad – a lifelong mountain enthusiast – would dig out new titles for me every week. I read *The White Spider*, Heinrich Harrer's account of death, hardship and eventual success on the Eiger. I pored over the map of the mountain's north face, learning each pitch, each crux and danger. There was the Hinterstoisser Traverse, crossed first by a man who swung and leaped boldly on his rope. There was the place where stone fall was most dangerous, where men were often felled by a single blow. There was the observational tunnel, that strange viewing window out into snow and ice from the tunnel where the train passed through. Then there was the place Toni Kurz froze on his rope and died, metres from salvation, his rescuers reaching out for him. There was a grim excitement in even these stories. I sketched the Eiger on my bedroom wall, tried to imagine how steep it was, what it would feel like to cling and shelter there. Through Harrer's prose, I became an armchair adventurer, each paragraph flooding me with adrenaline.

My dad steered me towards books by women, Julie Tullis and Lynn Hill. He wanted me to see that there were female role models in the mountains, that literature could be rich and varied, something close to my ordinary life. The cover of *Regions of the Heart*, the biography of Alison Hargreaves, showed the flanks of K2 in Pakistan, jagged and severe, cloud streaming behind. I gaped at it, traced its shape with my fingers. I opened the book. It was framed with a quote from Geoffrey Winthrop Young, mountaineer and poet. Winthrop Young describes 'a region of heart's desire' that is saved for mountain wildness, for 'the silvery glacier fire' and shadow, howling winds and streams. His words made me think of Robert Frost's 'Fire and Ice', a poem that has compelled me, almost haunted me since I first learned it as a child. As I started the book, the words of the prologue began to merge with Frost's poem:

> For a few moments more Alison Hargreaves lingers in the dark shelter of her tent.
>
> *Some say the world will end in fire,*
> *Some say in ice.*
>
> Her mind is racing with excitement.
>
> *From what I've tasted of desire*
> *I hold with those who favor fire.*
>
> She imagines her hands inside her multi-layered mittens grasping her ice axe, its shaft scratched and worn from use.

But if it had to perish twice,
I think I know enough of hate . . .

She hears the rasp of her breathing, the constant haul of her lungs on the depleted oxygen.

To say that for destruction ice
Is also great
And would suffice.

She zips the door shut, and goes out into the darkness of the early morning to climb the mountain.

It is fire which drives climbers, but it is ice which finishes them. Ice which proves itself sufficient.

When Alison was eight, her father John took her and her older sister, Susan, up Snowdon, the highest mountain in Wales. Though he'd planned to stick to the easiest, wide trails, a whiteout descended, the peak shrouded in mist, and they found themselves on the knife-edge of Crib Goch. Alison wasn't even wearing proper walking boots, but the exposure didn't faze her. When I was 15, I climbed

Snowdon via Crib Goch with my dad. We'd hiked in Scotland and Wales before, but this was my first introduction to really rocky terrain, places where I had to use my hands for support, haul myself up, knowing that a slip would be heart-stopping. I raced ahead of my father. My fear soon gave way to intent concentration, the texture of the rock, the sound of rain on the hood of my cagoule. I was addicted. I can imagine Alison's unbridled joy as she navigated through the mist, trusting the next foot placement and handhold. Scrambling is utterly absorbing. Like me, she cut her teeth in Scotland, ascending Ben Nevis and other Munros as a child. When she was 13, she did her first roped rock climb at the Roaches, the imposing brown gritstone edge that borders Staffordshire. The steepness made her stomach swoop, she gripped too hard with her hands. But her movements soon became fluid. And as she gained height, an almost eerie calm settled in her limbs.

She began to rock climb every weekend. When she wasn't climbing she was studying the Ordnance Survey map, learning the names of its sacred places: Black Rocks, High Tor, Raven Tor. Stanage Edge, Burbage, Kinder Scout. From the age of 11, she kept a diary where she recorded each local adventure in neat, round handwriting, her tone strangely mannered. Like me, she may have pored over the names of rock climbs, paused when she reached the strangest ones, savoured them, their surreal quality: Dithering Frights. Divine Providence. Don't Fluff It. Fading Star. She thought of what it would be to christen one herself. The Unprintable. Unthinkable. Wall of Sound. What it would mean to leave her mark on the landscape. When she climbed near Cromford, she found that the rock was scored with graffiti, people carving their names, love hearts and underlinings. She placed her hands in the initials of strangers. She did not need to carve her own name. With her body, she was writing Derbyshire, a quivering line, climbing steadily, moving across the page. And as I read about her childhood, she climbed into my head, moved steadily through my imagination.

Like Alison, my early relationship to mountains was mediated by my dad, though my love for rock and earth came from something earlier, from my mother, her gardens and allotments, her knowledge of vegetables, her ability to make anything grow. I spent Saturdays watching her dig and lift, plant potatoes and sow beans. Our car was always full of manure from local farms. She did all the heavy work herself and made the hard labour of it seem tender, almost elegant. Though I never helped as much as I should have, refused to follow in her boot-steps, I was shaped by the way she spoke about the rectangles of ground she cultivated. It seemed to me that exhausting herself in its service brought her relief. The sweetcorn and peas and carrots, the water-jewelled strawberries on the kitchen table: they were all hers. She studied the land around our house and my dad looked out beyond it. My father was no rock climber, but he was obsessed by hills, by the Scottish Munros and the wild landscapes of Torridon and Assynt, Rannoch Moor and Skye. Our house was stuffed with log books and maps, panoramic views of snow-laced summits, framed pictures taken from mountain calendars. When the school holidays came around and he finished teaching in the Mosborough school where he was head of English, my dad would pack his rucksack and take the train to Glasgow, then on towards Fort William. And when I became a teenager, I was finally allowed to go with him.

On our first trip, we stayed at a bunkhouse in Tulloch overlooking the railway, then set out to climb the Easians, two angular Munros above Loch Treig. In Derbyshire dialect, 'un' means 'one', so I translated 'Easi-uns' as 'the easy ones', thinking my dad had planned a steady introductory climb. We had no car and the most direct way to reach the hills was to walk along the railway tracks. I was nervy, always looking over my shoulder for trains. But when we saw the mountains, I forgot everything but sharpness and heather, the faint footpath gesturing towards the first summit. I set off too quickly, almost jogging. Halfway up, I was doubled over, leaning on a boulder to rest, huffing, 'I thought you said these were the easy ones.' My dad laughed. All week, I raced up the hills like a collie, always coming back to my father, to our calm companionship, to hearty stews for dinner and him nursing a pint of hoppy ale.

Because I had no brothers or sisters, I was son and daughter to him, companion and friend. John Hargreaves had the same kind of close relationship with Alison, loving her quiet determination, her stubbornness, the calm she experienced in the vertical world. He was described as undemonstrative, quiet. But they spoke through slopes and summits, the language of navigation. There's a photograph of her on Bunster Hill in Derbyshire as a tot, duffel coat clad and in a woollen hat, her face crumpled into a grin. It reminds me of a photo of me in the Lake District aged six, windswept and alert, a day when I apparently spent the whole climb from the valley floor arguing with my parents about why I shouldn't be made to wear my jacket. I quarrelled so doggedly that I won. Though I was young, I can almost remember it, how keenly I longed for the wind on my skin, how ordinary things like coats and hats and food became unimportant to me when I was in the mountains. Though I relied on my body to propel me up the hills, mountains have always made me feel strangely untethered, light, freed and unselfconscious.

To know the lure of the Peak District – the place where Alison and I both learned to climb – you have to slog your way up to its gritstone edges and traverse the hillside, walking directly underneath them, cleaving to the line of the rock. It's only then that you appreciate the drama of Derbyshire outcrops. From a distance, they look mild and inviting: stone waves, crashing benevolently towards the land. They are seldom more than 100 feet high. But from below, they swell and bulge and rear over you, looming green and grey, crosshatched by shadow. There are overhangs and dank corners, imposing slabs and jagged flakes. At dusk, they are like an empty stage, eerie with silence. Staring up at them, you imagine the dramas they've hosted, climbers like Alison testing themselves against friction, holding on for dear life. Gritstone is a kind of sandstone. I remember learning about it in school before I ever understood what it was. Sedimentary rock, tight-packed grains. I used to say the word aloud. Grit. It's utter hardness in the mouth, as if you're holding a tiny piece of grey rock on your tongue, running it over the roughness. Porous. Strongly cemented. Weak and strong layers. I knew the properties of gritstone before I understood what it was like to place my palms flat on a ledge of it and make a strange move called a 'mantelshelf', hoisting my body up awkwardly, what it was like to reach high at the top of a route and grope for a hold, not knowing if I'd find one.

Already in love with hillwalking, my first outdoor rock climb was on Stanage Edge, the long, curled lip of gritstone that overlooks the Hope Valley, high above the fringes of Sheffield. It was a route called Flying Buttress, less than 20 metres long, but every move felt precarious, thrilling. I remember the smooth slab at the beginning, how it seemed as if I was trusting my feet on nothing. Climbing teaches you to have faith in your own body and in the surface of the earth. It grounds you, even as you move into the air. The afternoon we chose was hot, stifling, with a cobalt-blue sky that made anything feel possible. The route was an easy grade, ideal for a beginner, but it was so much harder than I'd expected: the angles forbidding, the rock chafing my hands, the trees and bracken below shelving away from me. I struggled and swore, sweated and grumbled. But when I finally hauled myself over the top, the whole of my childhood landscape was spread out before me. I was breathless and giddy, buffeted by the wind. This was an adventure you could have any Sunday, testing yourself against steepness. I was hooked.

There is poetry in the world of Derbyshire climbing. Every name suggests a drama and a cast. Thrombosis. Rigor Mortis. Beady Eye. On a Wing and a Prayer. I love the morose ones best, the dark humour of them. Vanishing Point. Gathering Gloom. Off With His Head. Some can only be said with a grimace. Savage Amusement. Melancholy Witness. Agony Crack. I love each one, their promise and foreboding. Heaven Crack. Hell Crack. Blue December Sky. Imagine naming a route for yourself, earning the right by climbing it for the first time. Imagine the possibility and fear of it. All language yours. Devil's Chimney. Fading Star. The Ashes. Stay in the Light. At Stanage, there is even a Hargreaves' Original route which I climbed once in winter, teetering my way up the bold slab. It is nothing to do with Alison, I learned later, but named after Albert Hargreaves who made the first ascent in 1928. When you climb gritstone, you climb in the polished recesses of history.

From her first routes, Alison's prodigious talent for climbing was undeniable. Her teenage years were a haze of day trips and battered down jackets, hitchhiking round the country with her best mate and frequent climbing partner, Bev England. In the 1970s, rock climbing was experiencing a rapid surge in popularity, indoor climbing walls opening for the first time, magazines filling the shops, their covers plastered with wiry men in Lycra levering themselves up overhangs. It was a kind of subversive counterculture, life on the road, van life, climbing by day and drinking by night. It must have been seductive. When she was still a teenager, Alison got a part-time job at the

Bivouac, an outdoor shop in Matlock Bath, a cave of ropes, tents and sleeping bags, all the enticing paraphernalia of the climbing, dirtbag life. Matlock Bath is a surreal clutch of shops and houses below the limestone escarpment of High Tor. A haven for bikers, all leather and noise, it's a seaside town without the sea, amusement arcades and chip shops, neon candy floss and illuminations.

The Bivoauc was run by Yorkshireman Jim Ballard: bearded, opinionated, in his early 30s. The son of a steel worker, Jim was a self-made man, bristling with confidence and worldliness. To a girl as excited by climbing as Alison, he must have been a compelling figure, the symbol of an adult world beyond the gatekeepers she was used to, teachers and parents who encouraged her to knuckle down at school and think about university and steady jobs beyond. He seemed to know everyone, had an anecdote for every occasion, treated the landscape as a friend. And no doubt he paid special attention to his new assistant, impressed by her liveliness, youthful optimism, her hunger for climbing stories. Alison was energetic, strong, beaming, hair piled messily on top of her head. As their friendship grew through their shared purpose in the shop, Jim began to take Alison on trips to

Wales, introducing her to friends, to the glamour of adult conversation, dinner parties and long drives. Everyone admired her intelligence, her commitment to climbing. In turn, Alison was impressed by Jim's personal freedom: he was his own boss, taking off to Europe whenever he wanted. I imagine her watching him from behind the counter in the shop as he joked with customers, noticing his shoulders, the line of his jaw, the pitch of his voice as if for the first time.

On the morning after her 18th birthday, Alison faced her parents across the breakfast table, bags packed at her feet: she was leaving to stay with Jim at his house overnight. His wife, Jean, had left him and she intended to keep him company. They were shocked, but they were powerless to stop her. Days passed and Alison did not return home. Her mother rang Jim Ballard. As her biographers tell it:

> He passed the telephone to Alison. Her words struck her mother like hammer blows. Alison said she had been unhappy at home for many months. Jim was her lover, and she intended to stay with him permanently.

When I first read that, I kept thinking of a line by the poet Julia Copus: 'We don't fall in love: it rises through us/ the way that certain music does.' Love as a seeping, inevitable sensation. I think of a teenage girl, idolising an adult and all he symbolised, united to him by a shared purpose, a sense of freedom in landscape, not wanting to separate the man from the world he showed her. Copus's poem is wry and the ending undercuts the opening sentiment: the inevitability of new love is something we just convince ourselves of, a story we tell ourselves. But it remains a compelling one. Perhaps it is our favourite story.

Stubborn, purposeful, Alison was as committed to her plan as she was to climbing. She moved into Jim's house in the hills, Meerbrook Lea. She'd always excelled at school, but she wanted to burst out of the classroom and run free: to spend day after day testing herself on the brutal routes of the Peak District, coming home with scuffed knuckles and bruised elbows, grinning and windswept. With Ballard, she relished the adult life she was suddenly part of. There would be monotony, bills and housework and the clunking gears of everyday life, but she did not feel them just yet. She spent days on end roaming the moors with their collie, Rupert. She wanted to merge with the heather and rock.

Life gathered pace at Meerbrook Lea, her happiness waxed and waned. Alison had experienced significant changes while she was still a teenager. She had missed the opportunities afforded by higher education and been plunged into a new domestic routine. From their stone cottage nestled in the Derwent Valley, she had access to the limestone crags that lay beyond, but she also took on much of the physical work of the house as well as helping Jim with the finances, and making gear for climbers on an industrial-sized sewing machine at home. She cooked, cleaned and manufactured gear, all within the walls of Meerbrook Lea. Her social circle shrank. She only kept in touch with her climbing partner and old friend Bev England intermittently. One of Jim's friends is quoted in *Regions of the Heart* describing her as a girl who had 'led a very sheltered life', a life structured around climbing and who 'didn't seem old for her years'.

In February 1988, around the time of her 26th birthday, Alison was feeling nauseous, her mornings dizzy and green. She took a pregnancy test. It was positive. Jim and

Alison married and took a day-long honeymoon on the North York Moors, squeezing in a climb. Alison was resolutely determined to remain active through her pregnancy. Even as she became heavier, more tired, she continued her training, leading up to her notorious climb on the Eiger Nordwand when she was six months pregnant, a feat which shocked the world. Less than three and a half months from the birth of her child, she was on the notorious Hinterstoisser Traverse, the great airy step into the unknown I'd read about in Harrer's books, with her climbing partner, Steve Aisthorpe. The Eiger north face or Nordwand is nicknamed the 'Mordwand' – 'murder wall' – because of its body count. It is not the most difficult climb in the Alps, but it is vast and dark, soaring dramatically above the Swiss hamlet of Kleine Scheidegg. It is a cauldron for storms and a place of stone fall, rocks shearing off and sailing through the air. Alison was gambling not only with her own life, but with the life of her foetus. On the trip, she was dogged by low moods and lethargy. As Ed Douglas and David Rose report it, her climbing partner, Steve, observed, 'Alison didn't look pregnant at the start of the climb but she did at the end.' Still, they were successful. Alison was both elated and vindicated. She would remain a mountaineer until the end. Home in Derbyshire, Alison felt the first twinges of labour when she was out climbing at Black Rocks in Cromford. She continued paying out the rope for Jim before suggesting they should go to the hospital. I cannot imagine such calm acceptance. She had climbed until the very last second.

In the first trimester of pregnancy, I told myself I felt too sick to climb. I rolled with nausea, feeling the whole sea inside me. I went to Cornwall to teach a creative writing course and plunged into the ocean every day, wincing, the coldness briefly shocking me out of my stupor. I wasn't sure if this was pure morning sickness – that strange misnomer, for it lasts all day – or a side effect of coming off the antidepressants that I'd taken faithfully for years, two little capsules of Sertraline a day to stop me from whittling a rough stone of anxiety into a smooth, hard marble that could rattle around my head for ever. Pregnancy was a chance to wean myself off the drugs. But it was also a time of immense, inevitable anxiety, the first lonely months with their silence, monitoring and secrecy. Perhaps I was just too nervous to climb. I hated the idea of a harness over my belly. My shape was barely altered, but I imagined the cargo of my womb, couldn't bear anything to hold my stomach too tightly. Worse, I was afraid of falling, as if the shock could jolt my baby out of me. I stopped going out to Stanage Edge, made excuses to my climbing partners. For a while, I still trained at the bouldering wall close to my house in Sheffield, a place of short routes, neon artificial holds and safety mats to cushion the fall. I was exhausted, distracted. I planned domestic projects instead, painting my partner's house, buying plants with wide leaves.

I was also accommodating my new body. All my life, I'd wanted to be a line. As a ten-year-old, I was stocky and strong, built like a Shetland pony. I loved food, devouring loaves of bread on their own in the garden on Saturday afternoons, biting off huge chunks, grazing on cheese and apples late at night. I ate happily, zealously, spent my pocket money on fizzy sweets, asked for seconds whenever they were offered. I was also active, brought up to walk half-marathon distances from as soon as I was able to. I loved swimming and cycling, trudging up hills in bad weather. I was substantial, round-cheeked and muscular. I looked like a weathered cherub. But one day in Year 7, a willowy girl called me fat across the table in food technology, giggling into her hands. *Fat. Fat. Fat.* I could smell pizzas baking in the ovens behind us. I had layered mine so carefully: cheese, tomato, green peppers, slivers of salami. My cheeks burned red. When I wore cycling shorts, I felt wobbly, outsized. My dance teacher tapped my bottom lightly as I stood at the barre on Monday nights in leggings and a leotard, forcing my feet into first position. *Let's get rid of that bum.*

I began to exercise at home: aerobics workouts to blaring pop songs, star jumps and sit-ups. I had never been unfit. At school, we took a 'bleep test', a fitness exam to test endurance. In the echoing sports hall, a building that always looked too new for the rest of the school, we had to run lengths of the basketball court from line to line, keeping up with a shrill beep. As the test carried on, the gaps between the sounds became shorter. When you were most tired, you had to push yourself harder. As the levels increased, the other children sloped off one by one, or flopped onto the ground behind the goal, clutching their chests. My limbs tingled. I was aware of being more and more alone, but I barely looked around me. I focused on my plimsolls slapping against the hard floor, the urgent, plaintive sound of them. I was in a tunnel, flanked by my loud blood, my full lungs. Eventually, there were only two of us left, me and David, a grim pixie of a boy with an ear piercing, a 30-a-day smoking habit and a fondness for throwing chairs. Afterwards, the PE teacher took us to one side and asked if we would represent the school in the local athletics championships.

I trained for weeks. Laps of the cricket pitch near my house, behind the pub where my dad drank every Sunday, where I used to look forward to salt-and-vinegar crisps and lemonade sucked up through a pink straw. I timed myself with a stopwatch. There was a steep bank that I could run up, only a few metres high, but it became my private mountain. I sprinted up it, over and over, stumbling on the rough tussocky ground, loving the burn in my thighs and calves. I felt leaner, sharper. On the day of the race, I was fidgety and giddy, giggling at the slightest provocation. As we filed towards the bus that would ferry us to the local athletics track, Mr Coleman took me to one side.

'I've changed the team for the 800 metres around slightly. Caroline will run for the school and you'll run as her reserve. That's OK, isn't it?'

Only one runner – the nominated athlete – from each school would score in the race. The reserve wasn't in the competition. I would not be racing. I would be running for fun. I nodded grimly. I let the clamour of the coach journey swirl around me. When we arrived at the stadium – a scrappy cinder track with some peeling green benches positioned round it – I sat alone on the bench, lacing up my spikes. On the start line, I was ushered into the second row. The faster girls were to go ahead. They were thin, sinewy and hard-faced, hair pulled back into ponytails or braided and pinned to their scalps. Stick drawings of girls. We all leaned forward intently, angling our bodies towards the distance ahead. Sometimes, a leg would twitch slightly, or someone would start forwards, anticipating the gun. When it finally fired, the shot rent the air. We were jostling, pushing, feral, sprinting into the first bend, trying to get clear of one another. I have always disliked crowds. The only child in me wants to open up a distance. My legs began to carry me away from Caroline, away from the girls I'd started with. I could see the leader, legs like scissors, upright and composed, striding towards the stands. I imagined I was climbing a mountain, the summit inching into view. As the bell rang to signal the last lap, I realised I was in second place. My legs felt wobbly, elastic, lactic acid creeping through my whole body. Every breath was raw. I was dimly aware of Mr Coleman, clapping his hands violently, the whistle round his neck swinging. *Don't look back.* I did not. I imagined that the track was carrying me, that I was only being rolled around it by gravity, pushed forwards by an invisible hand. I ran past the trees that flanked Baden Powell Road, branches touching and separating in the wind. I wanted to be moved like them. Then the home straight, the swell of cheering from my school, kids jumping up and down on their rucksacks. I burst across the line and crumpled with nausea. I was second, just behind the leader. It was my first race.

As I ran, year on year, my body lessened. The miles all became part of one infinite race, I barely noticed the gaps between training sessions. I ran on the fells until I vomited with effort. My shoulders had two hard notches protruding from them and I used to touch them obsessively, proof of my new shape. My dance teacher remarked that I could do with putting on some weight. 'Men don't like a skeleton,' my friends said. I ran. I swam. I did 100 sit-ups before bed. I was becoming linear. All my life, I've approached the mirror warily, the way you would an animal that you don't want to startle. I've stood in front of my reflection and run my hands down my hips, over the tops of my legs as if trying to smooth out a sheet. I've longed to flatten myself, to be tall and stately as a tree. Whenever I'm depressed or angry or rejected, I punish myself with Ryvita and avocado, daily runs that get longer and longer, climb higher and higher. In 2015, I trained so hard for the London Marathon I barely slept, pounding the pavements around Ecclesall Road at 4am and 5am. I was trying to break three hours, a near-elite time for a woman. I don't remember the race. All I saw was the ribbon of the tarmac, the line I'd drawn for myself in the sand, the single track of my need. I crossed the finishing line delirious. My watch showed two hours, 59 minutes and 59 seconds.

To become a mother, I had to renounce lines. I could not be a path any more, an arrow or a track, underlining the desires of others. My body was softening, filling, ripening. I needed to learn how to hold, how to contain. In the shower, with the water reddening my skin, I looked down at the new roundness of my breasts, the punctuation of my nipples, the blue veins under the surface. My stomach began to curve, growing every day, eager, as if it wanted me to take up more space in the world. As my bump grew, it entered every room before me, announcing itself. My face became fuller. The skin of my abdomen stretched taut, tight as a drum. I bloomed into the second trimester, then the third. Then, my bump was a fullness I could cradle. I felt voluptuous, carved in marble. I began to love tight-fitting clothes, black dresses that showed off my new shape. My silhouette was more interesting. At night, the baby squirmed and dived. I felt as if it was scuttling inside me, dancing, cavorting. I could not remember what it was to be straight, flat-chested, stippled with muscle. I groaned with heaviness, a branch sagging on a tree. At night I lay on my left side with a pillow between my knees and couldn't sleep for my cargo. I felt that I was becoming circular, no beginning or end. I was the sun, fierce over the Hope Valley on a still day, coaxing out climbers. My mind became less angular too. I no longer felt gripped by purpose, let my thoughts swirl like fish in a tank, underwater. I often thought of Alison, my ghost companion, dreamed of her bivouacking on the Eiger with her baby kicking inside. Jess was enchanted by the inwardness of it all, my belly teeming with life. Outside in his garden, frogs shimmied around the small pond, dense with gratitude.

I'd also cut through the line that connected me to rock climbing. Right up until I became pregnant, I had continued climbing with Andrew, slate quarries in Wales and limestone crags in Derbyshire, steady as two craftsmen. In the decade or so since we'd met, our relationship had flickered on and off, on and off again. We'd danced around each other, friends then partners then friends, always keeping our amicable companionship, our shared purpose in the mountains, our respect for one another. Mainly, we just climbed. No matter how far I ranged, the rope that linked us, that thin line of safety, was still there, anchoring me, bringing me back to the mountains and to our friendship, breathless, tired and afraid. It was both complicated and not. But motherhood was something new, something other.

The pub I met him in that night in April smelled of dogs and pork scratchings, the jukebox too loud. Andrew sat wrapped in his black down jacket. His hair was cropped close as if he was ready for an expedition. He was drinking Easy Rider. I nursed my Diet Coke, watching bubbles travel up the glass and break against the surface. The light made me feel sick, as almost everything did at the time: smells, tastes, motion, stasis. We talked about Kalymnos in Greece, the roadside crags and wide sea, the caves and humidity, the goats who steal climbers' sandwiches. We planned mythical sport climbing holidays, routes in the morning and beer in the afternoon. We joked about the misadventures of our friends, sprained limbs and fondue. I asked about his training, the finger board he'd built in his house to improve his strength, practising pull-ups in the evening while his cat watched curiously from the windowsill. It was so easy. We laughed. He got another round. I thought about not telling him. When I spoke, I could feel the rope between us going slack, the fraying, the letting go. In the silence, I felt for it and there was nothing there.

'Congratulations. It's what you've always wanted,' he said. He smiled kindly. I fumbled for my car keys. He took his rucksack and set off into the evening.

'Where are you going?' I called to no one. And I heard the answer I feared in the silence.

'Climbing.'

/\/\/\ FIRST LEDGE

Belaying is the part you like best: facing the valley, noting the flight paths of birds, feeling the wind as it paws your face, getting to know the contours of you, wide nose, strong chin, thick eyebrows. When you climb, you lean into the landscape, but here it leans into you. Your feet dangle over the edge and you kick them against the rock, swinging your legs in space. You're an eagle and the belay stance is your eyrie, cluttered with all the things you consider precious, tools that shine, eye-bright. The feathers in your jacket keep you warm. You've often stood on the edge of Stanage and imagined spreading your arms out like the *Angel of the North*, dipping forwards and taking flight. On Mam Tor, you once saw a paraglider taking off. Up close, it was a gaudy marvel, the mechanics of liftoff. Airborne, the man became a speck, carried by currents, an Icarus heading for the heavens.

You remember it from school. *This is the story of a boy who flew too close to the sun. A boy whose wings were made of wax and feathers. This is the story of wax melting, down falling to earth, a parent with empty hands. This is the story of a boy who burned too bright.*

You keep your attention on the rope, keeping it taut. Not tight exactly, but snug. Pull. Relax. Take in slack. Your nose is running and you want to reach up a hand but you can't take them from the double rope, yellow strand and blue strand. Your knuckles are slightly red. When it's bitter, the tips of your fingers turn pale and numb, a tinge inherited from your grandfather. There is a pleasant rhythm to belaying from above, matching the second's pace, the ropes coiling at your side.

There are clouds massing in the west. A fat raindrop strikes your cheek, then suddenly you're hunkering down as a squall of rain travels over you. It goes as soon as it came, ushered on by the wind. In Great Langdale, something is always breaking, changing, opening. The clouds meet the mountains and give the summits everything they carry, turn out their pockets. You love its solemn character, its short temper.

Your shoes hurt. You should have taken them off when you set up the anchor. You think of Gwen Moffat climbing barefoot here, moving over these same slabs and knowing their roughness with her toes, the leathery soles of her feet. You think of her climbing with men, out-climbing all of them, hear her voice, always half amused and throaty:

> On the first morning, I took them up Middlefell Buttress: five of us, all on one rope. It was slow, cold and boring. They climbed faster than I did, surrounded with an almost visible aura of masculine resentment. So I took them to Gwynne's Chimney on Pavey Ark, and as they struggled and sweated in that smooth cleft, sparks flying from their nails, and me waiting at the top with a taut rope and a turn around my wrist, I knew that I had won.

This is Middlefell Buttress. It is slow and cold. But you do not know how to be bored in the mountains. You would not be one of those men. You would pitch yourself towards the sky with glee, let bad weather fill the tent of your body and shake you. You would climb with Gwen.

VERTIGO

The rope pulls tight. What shall we call
this new thing we're about?
These days we live in taking
care and chances. Why name it?
My heart is in my mouth as I shout Climbing . . .

– Andrew Greig

2020

I'm three feet off the ground when I realise I've been holding my breath. I exhale and the wind whips away whatever I was keeping inside. It is a clear day, fiercely cold. The sky over Stanage is taut, expectant, not quite afternoon, not quite evening. It has a pinkish tinge. I imagine the sun crossing it carefully, anxiously like a man on a slack line, teetering above thin air. I think of a tanned, lean athlete like Dean Potter stepping into the sky, his feet on a line of flat webbing, 3,000 feet above the ground in Yosemite. I can see the blue shadows on the spires of rock, the orange gape of the ground, his muscles tightening with balance, a vein pulsing in his neck. I hear the echo of a single stone falling, miles below. He wears no safety lanyard, no harness to attach him to the line, no parachute strapped to his back. A slip could turn his body into a stone. Dean Potter is dead now. He didn't slip high-lining. He never put a foot wrong. He was killed attempting an illegal proximity wingsuit flight from Taft Point above Yosemite Valley, crashing into the rock, meeting it head on. He did not fall to his death, his death rushed to meet him. But it's the slackline I'm preoccupied with as I climb, the space on either side of his body, the imperative not to look down. I try to blink the image away. Don't think of him. I am in Derbyshire. I am safe, tied onto a rope. I am climbing outdoors for the first time in two years.

Gritstone has a special way of humiliating you. The starts are the worst, the sense that you'll never lever your body off the ground. Non-existent footholds, niches polished by use, turned to glass. High reaches to uncertain, sloping ledges. Forbidding corners that you have to hoist yourself round. I have forgotten this, forgotten how to use my body. I have been softened by nursing, by the salty smell of my son's head and the warmth of his cheek. My hands are delicate again and the grit has already made me bleed. We're at High Neb, the quiet end of the edge, on a route called Typhoon that weaves its way under a huge bulge of rock and darts over a steep overhang. I am seconding, the rope always above me, my partner bracing and holding me if I slip.

Leading is precarious, a test of nerve. In trad climbing, the first climber sets out alone with the rope trailing behind them. Their protection comes from gear that they push into gaps and crevices in the rock. There are cams, strange alligator-like contraptions with a spring mechanism that expand when you release a trigger, and nuts, solid metal shapes of different sizes that you wiggle into place and pull down on, making sure they stay put. Only once the leader has clipped their rope through the gear are they relatively safe, hoping it would brace a fall. Even so, a bad placement could move or rip out. The leader is always facing the prospect of hitting the ground. But once they've reached the top and set up a secure belay, their partner can climb in safety, the rope going tight above them as they move. The worst scenario for me is that I dangle in space, frustrated and tired, a comical pendulum above the Hope Valley. I approach the bulge of rock, the place where I have to traverse left, lean back to manoeuvre around it. My hands are completely numb from the cold. They feel swollen, ballooning from my wrists. I have no idea what I'm holding on to, whether I have a secure purchase or not. I feel my feet slipping. I remind myself that I am secure.

As a second, your only real fear is that you won't be caught. Most of the time, it is completely irrational. Climbing like this is an exercise in trust: your partner will hold you, stop you. Yet I am afraid, legs shaking. From the ground, the bulge looked innocuous, a protrusion in the rock, easily negotiated. Up close, it is vast and grotesque. It forces me to cower, awkward and ungainly. It is not like the swell of a pregnant belly. It is tumorous, misshapen, looming. I stand on a small ledge, panting, and retrieve a nut from above me. It's jammed tight, utterly stuck and everything I seem to do only makes it more firmly wedged. As I rattle and tug at it, I feel unstable, every movement risking a slip. I swear, breathing too heavily. When I finally yank it out, I clip it to my harness. Now there is nothing to distract me from the move I have to make, stepping out onto a slab, moving awkwardly under the bulge. I rehearse it in my mind. I look for secure footholds, try to visualise what I'm stepping towards, but there's hardly anything there. The route trends left and finishes diagonally upwards from me, so a slip here would see me swing violently into the air. I am safe, but it doesn't feel like safety. Most of all, I am intimidated, humbled by this body of rock, by the hunched mass of it, the terrifying solidity of it, its tenacity and roughness, how it has stood, unmoved, and received our worship, centuries of touch. It sees my fear and gives it back to me. It is a dank, mossy mirror and I do not like what I see.

I flick the yellow rope over the bulge so that it runs straight above me. Routes like this demand two ropes to avoid drag. I am doubly tied, doubly protected. I test the air with my foot and then draw it back again. I look down and High Neb seems dark and angular, near deserted. The wind plucks at me. I talk to myself, a mutter first, then an anguished yell. *Come on. Come on.* I jam my right hand further into the rock. *Get on with it.* Then, the movement draws me in and

I'm away, alive, fluid. I'm on the slab now and moving fast, climbing up. Adrenaline courses through me, hot and slick. But I am weary. This is the last climb of the day and the muscles in my forearms throb. And now I'm beneath the overhang. I need all my strength to pull myself up. I try and fall, try and fall. I howl with anguish. I want to punch myself, slap myself, make my numb face hurt. Then a tightening comes over me. It is like chiffon scarves, one being pulled tight over my face and another then another being crammed down my throat, into my lungs. I cannot breathe. I weep and heave. I hang on the rope, in space. I am nowhere. Above me, my partner is calm and steady. I hear a level voice from the top of the crag. *I've got you. It's OK. Just breathe. Breathe. I can lower you whenever you want.* It is a soft voice, a strong voice. It belongs to Andrew.

When I'm back on the ground, Andrew abseiling down to retrieve his gear, I face the weak, lemony sunset, the cold sky, the familiar browns and tans of the open moors, flattened when I try to take a picture. Photographs never capture what is particular about landscape, what captivates. My tears fall into the heather and vanish. The panic attack has left me feeling light, insubstantial. I pull my down jacket around me, teeth chattering uncontrollably. Andrew is busy with the ropes. I am useless, inert. I cannot look at him.

'I'm such a fucking embarrassment.'

'You could never embarrass yourself in front of me.'

I know this to be true and this stings me. We pick our way down through the millstones, some of them bright with spray paint, graffitied smiles. We lose the path for a while and bog saps our energy. We don't speak.

For me, motherhood is like a permanent state of slacklining, highlining. I have forgotten what it is to feel confidence. In her memoir *My Wild and Sleepless Nights*, Clover Stroud describes the first few weeks with a new baby as the most perfect time:

> Those first two weeks are . . . like magic, since mothering in its most intense, consuming, tender sense is all that occupies the days. The demands of the world are away.

Though I felt that surge of tenderness when we ferried Alfie home for the first time – tiny in his car seat – it was trepidation and bewilderment that presided in those early days, not magic. I would swaddle him in blankets and lie gazing at him, amazed that he had come from my body, terrified that the vastness of the world would break him, his body too light for its angles and edges. I lay on the bed in his yellow nursery, a parade of pastel animals marching round the walls, and wept with the new loneliness I felt, the terror of love and responsibility.

Jess was calm with Alfie, relaxed and confident with his small shape. He'd lie him on a sheepskin rug in front of the fire, lean over him and play guitar, looping refrains that had him mesmerised. That was how we were, all of us on the living-room floor, when the midwife called in for a check-up. She was gentle as she accepted tea, then told me off for making it. I showed her Alfie's latch, mustered the energy to speak, describing his feeding patterns as she scribbled in her notebook. I was anxious to show her that I was doing a good job. My nipples felt raw, but I tried not to wince as Alfie rooted and suckled. When it was time for her to examine him, I could barely let go of him. He had lived inside my body for nine months, seeing someone else's hands on him was still a shock. On the weighing scales, he mewled and wriggled. Then she held him up to the light.

'He looks a bit yellow still. I think he's jaundiced. We'd better send you to the Royal to be checked.'

Barely two days after we'd left the hospital, we were driving back in the early winter dark. Rain pelted the windscreen, furious with us. Jess parked on a verge and the car got stuck, wheels spinning hopelessly in the mud. We had to abandon it. Inside the maze of the Nightingale Ward, we descended to the basement, picked our way through corridors, following other worried parents. In the children's ward, the walls were pasted with crayon drawings and draped with tinsel. A huge Christmas tree shimmered in the corner. The doctors and nurses were intently cheerful. We waited in a conservatory, with a view of the main ward. Two parents with a newborn were watching TV, bored. A doctor chided them for leaving their baby on the bed. 'You must hold him,' he said earnestly. 'Always hold him.' Next to them, an emaciated teenage girl clutched her knees and scrolled through her phone. Her mother was bird-like and dark under the eyes, darting out to the conservatory to get reception, having angry conversations. 'She's asking for you. She won't agree to treatment until you come.' Her breathing was quick and sharp. 'I didn't want to bother you, but she's insisting. She wants her dad.'

From her bed, the girl tossed her phone away angrily and flopped back onto the pillows. I could not stop watching the mother, her restless pacing, her gaunt face reflected in the windowpanes. I tried not to imagine her days earlier, opening the door of her daughter's bedroom, seeing the empty bottle of pills, sensing a stillness on the duvet. I held Alfie close and rocked him.

Our doctor was young with gel-spiked hair and huge square glasses, bright red frames. At first, I thought he was ostentatious, then realised with sudden pity that they were probably to cheer up the children. When he crouched down with a needle to take a sample of Alfie's blood – a droplet from his tiny red heel – I felt my jaw clench. Watching my baby's skin being punctured made a new gap in the fabric of our world together. I felt the pinch and throb, tensed at his thin cry. The doctor ushered us to a private room, lit intense blue, the colour of a gas flame. The curtains were drawn. There was a narrow single bed, a monitor turned to face the wall and a rectangular tank, pulsing with warm light. An incubator. I had never seen one in real life before, only in TV programmes and nightmares, visions of tiny newborns in intensive care. Alfie would be placed in the tank in his nappy and treated with

UV light. I have since learned that this technique was pioneered by Charles Warren, a medic who made three attempts on Everest in the 1930s, serving as expedition doctor on the 1938 attempt led by Bill Tilman. Thanks to Warren, neonatal jaundice is treated mainly by ultraviolet light rather than blood transfusions. The doctor explained how phototherapy works, his glasses pale in the blueness, something underwater about the whole scene.

I should not touch him, must not take him out except to feed him. I must change his nappy through the side of the tank and keep each one to be weighed. The process can take days, nobody knows how long. Jaundice is caused by a build-up of bilirubin, a waste material, in the blood. Symptoms include a yellow tinge to the skin and whites of the eyes, dark urine, and itchiness. It is common in winter babies like Alfie, born to dark mornings and early nightfall. When the doctor said 'bilirubin' I heard 'Billy Reuben', imagined a cowboy with guns slung around his waist, a Stetson and a checked shirt. Billy Reuben was riding on horseback through my son's veins, trampling him and leaving him yellow. When Alfie was placed inside the tank, he looked like a tiny astronaut. They slipped a little mask over his eyes, incongruously modern, as if he were some kind of voyager. Under the heat of the lamps, he stretched out, feline, and let the warmth touch his skin. At times, he looked like a man on a sunbed. I giggled and took photos, his long limbs reclining on his bed of towels. But when Jess left and the night shift started, fear settled in the pit of my stomach. First, Alfie had been safe inside me. Then, when he was born, I had held him close, fed him with my milk, barely put him down.

Now he was separate from me for the first time, abstract behind see-through walls, an exhibit. I could take him in: his long body and frog-like legs, the wisps of dark hair curling on his head, his grasping fingers and tiny nails. But all I wanted was to touch him. When he screamed to be fed, I leaped towards the incubator. The nurses had told me I could feed him with his mask on. *He won't mind as long as he can smell you.* But Alfie was outraged by his blindness, clawing at the eye mask, frantically scrabbling. He wanted to see me, needed to. I gently peeled it off and met his gaze, searching and serious. I held him to me and tried to make the feed last as long as possible. His body was like a loaf of just-baked bread. I did not want to put him back again. He wriggled and kicked, protested at the eye mask. In the tank, it kept slipping off. I rocked back and forth on the edge of my bed in the blue gloom.

Occasionally, I twitched the curtain to see the different darkness outside, imagining the lanes behind the hospital where I played for hours as a child, clambering through the hedgerows. I tried not to think of mothers with babies in intensive care because it made me weep for them. The giraffes on Alfie's muslin cloths upset me, their cheerful faces were too much. I had a bag full of books – Roxane Gay essays, a novel that had just won the Booker Prize – but I could not stomach the unfamiliar. Instead, I pulled out Alison Hargreaves's story, my well-thumbed copy of *Regions of the Heart*. It kept vigil with me through the night.

I was searching for Alison's experience of birth, wondering if she suffered as I did, if the pain floored her. I found few clues. Alison and Jim's son, Tom Ballard, was born in Belper in the autumn of 1988, a month of fire on the trees and on the ground. There is a black-and-white image of him as a small baby in Derbyshire – I came across it online and now I keep a copy of it in my book, a sort of bookmark. He's swaddled in white blankets like any other infant, his wrinkled face barely visible. But the mother who holds him is perched on the edge of a grit-stone lip, one leg stretched out in front of her. The photograph was taken at Black Rocks in Derbyshire, a surreal, brutal place to climb, the rock marked with graffiti at the top, name after name carved into its surface. I used to go there as a teenager and find other kids drinking cider at the top, bored kids from Matlock and Wirksworth hunkering down for the night with pills and cans. They ghost the photograph. Alison's face is serious, stark in white. Tom is just four days old, more or less the same age as incubator-bound Alfie. On our first day at home, I could barely carry him downstairs without my heart leaping, imagining myself dropping him, his tiny body breaking. The idea of being with him in a rocky place seemed unthinkable, abstract. But perhaps it was a failure of imagination on my part. Tom also looks content, safe, swaddled in the safety of his mother's arms. She is all he needs. He does not know where he is, but perhaps he senses the keenness of the air, the tickle of the breeze on his downy cheek.

*

What's certain to me is that Alison needed to be there, needed to return to Black Rocks. The pull to high reaches is difficult to explain to those who haven't felt it. Climbers and authors have exhausted themselves in the service of describing their desire. It is illogical, mysterious, contradictory. Time and again, lovers of mountaineering come back to George Mallory's description of climbing Everest, simultaneously trite and profound: 'Because it's there.' Robert Macfarlane puts it more starkly: 'Those who travel to mountain-tops are half in love with themselves, and half in love with oblivion.'

I have never liked to dwell on that sentiment too long, perhaps because I profoundly recognise it. The rock reminding me of my insignificance but bolstering my ego at the same time. Mountains renew our astonishment with the world. They doggedly endure, remind us that we are on earth only briefly. They pose disconcerting questions about the importance of our little plans and schemes. A black-and-white photo. A small woman and a tiny boy in a huge, sheer landscape, fathomless and steep. When we look up at mountains – look up to them – they humble us. It's easy to make them god-like. And perhaps it's easier to devote your life to the service of gods than humans. Giving yourself over to the care of your newborn pre-linguistic child is terrifying. There is instinct to guide you, but there is also the unshakable fear that you will get something wrong, that you will fail them, that you are somehow not enough. I have felt that same sense of inadequacy in mountains but without the accompanying vertigo, the swooping responsibility. When Alfie burbled and squirmed and murmured, I feared I didn't understand him, his face more inscrutable than rock.

In the early days of her son's life, Alison's devotion to Tom was unquestionable. She recorded his progress in her diary, her pride and delight when he sat up for the first time or took his first steps undeniable. And yet she often felt restless. Between the daily routine of nurture, naps and nappies, feeding and play, she longed for the carefree girl she used to be. As soon as she was able to leave Tom with her parents, she would escape for a few snatched hours – or even less – of soloing in the Peak District, climbing short routes without ropes, trying to maintain her fitness without wasting too much time away from her beloved son. I imagine it recharged her. But I also imagine her breasts filling with milk, skin tight, that uncomfortable, prickling sensation reminding her of Tom's need and her duty to fulfil it. Soloing was all she could manage between the demands of early motherhood, a few hours away to practise familiar moves, feel weather against her skin again.

I also wonder if she found herself more tentative, more cautious, her every movement considered. There are different levels of risk in climbing, but even the most innocuous activity in the mountains could be potentially fatal. When rock climbing started in the 19th century, in a party of climbers roped together it was simply assumed that the leader must not fall: any slip would mean hitting the ground. Over the decades, climbers have developed equipment to lessen the chances of this happening. The leader places protection wherever they can. The second stands below them and feeds the rope out through a friction device called a belay plate. If the leader falls, they should not (in theory) fall particularly far: their partner holds them tight on the rope, the protection placed in the rock holds too. But if there is a weak element in the chain – a poor piece of gear placement or nowhere to place gear at all, a crumbling piece of rock, a distracted belayer – the leader could come to grief. Climbing ropes are strong enough to hold extreme weight, but they are also stretchy.

As Ed Douglas and David Rose put it:

> The paradox is that it is precisely this element of responsibility, this awareness of what gravity may do if things go wrong, which makes climbing, and especially leading, such an intoxicating activity . . .

I have underlined this bit of the text. The lines became wobbly as I tried to draw them, the undulation of edges. They call back a memory of the first time I saw mountain rescue helicopters speeding to Stanage as I was walking down from the crag after a long day on gritstone. They made the air clank and hum, mechanical. Later, as I sat in the car eating my sandwiches, not quite ready to drive back to the city and the tedium of Sunday afternoon, my phone buzzed. It was my climbing partner, breathless and nervy. After I'd left, he'd stayed behind packing his bags when two bodies crumpled on the ground next to him, a woman and a man. He had to phone for help, staying with them, praying it would be quick. Later, he pieced the story together. It was a young woman out climbing with her uncle, one of her first times on rock. He was leading and she was seconding.

Attached to the rope, she slipped and fell, but his belay wasn't secure and the weight of her fall dragged them both down to the ground. Her pelvis was broken. If I had left just moments later, I would have witnessed the full horror of it. Whenever I see a collection for Edale Mountain Rescue, I drop some coins into the pot. A kind of insurance policy. I might need this one day.

I always tell myself that the worst dangers I face in Derbyshire are a broken leg or a few bruises. But there are deaths even here. The British Mountaineering Council states that it 'recognises that climbing, hill walking and mountaineering are activities with a danger of personal injury or death'. Each terrain, each style of climbing, brings its own risks. There are objective hazards from the environment: bad or rapidly changing weather, poor equipment, falling rocks, falling ice, avalanches, falls from ice slopes, falls down snow slopes, falls into crevasses and the dangers from altitude. Listing them feels dizzying. Then there are subjective hazards like a climber's poor judgement, poor planning, lack of skills, or inadequate conditioning. And judgement can be influenced by personal ambition, fear of the consequences of failure, perhaps simply being human, emotional rather than entirely rational. Sometimes, halfway up a route on the sharp end of the rope, I've felt overwhelmed by the sheer weight of responsibility, the sense that one slip could cost me everything. The more anxious I feel, the more likely I am to fall. You can will your own fears into existence.

Throughout her life, Alison was reluctant to admit the reality of these risks in public. She maintained that it was possible to eliminate danger through good judgement, experience and careful preparation. As a new mother, she was filmed soloing in Derbyshire, her body lithe in the cracks, her voice edited in: *If I was frightened I wouldn't go. If I thought it was extremely dangerous, I wouldn't do it.* She was softly spoken, measured and pragmatic, her voice level and calm. In interviews, when she talked about risk, she could come across as emotionless. *Look, I drive on motorways at night, I consider that risky.* It's a comparison I've often made myself, looking for reassurance. At the panel on motherhood and risk at the Banff Mountain Film and Book Festival in 1994, Alison implied that those who die in the mountains die because of poor judgement, being in the wrong place at the wrong time. Journalists often speculated that she must know no mortal fear, have no concept of her own death. But her biographers, Ed Douglas and David Rose, have a more nuanced understanding. In *Regions of the Heart*, they suggest that she did often have doubts about the safety of what she was undertaking, but she could not admit those agonies of indecision in public:

> She had guessed, like many high-altitude climbers, that it needed a mental trick to get up big mountains. You understood the risks and planned for them, but assumed that somehow they wouldn't apply to you.

Mountaineers – like any specialist in a field – conceive of risk differently. Alison knew that the majority of people who go climbing in the Himalaya do indeed come back alive and she was confident in her abilities: her fitness, her strength, her judgement, her fierce desire for life. What else is there? Much more. More that cannot be accounted for. Perhaps we all have to assume a certain kind of invulnerability simply to get on with the daily business of living. And risks and responsibilities are not specific to mothers. When she wrote her book about the loss of Joe Tasker, *Where the Mountain Casts Its Shadow*, Maria Coffey sensed she had crossed a line in the climbing community by being candid and open about the devastating effect mountaineering can have on a family. 'The world needs risk-takers,' she says. 'They inspire, challenge and encourage. They set off sparks, igniting fires that burn long after their passing. They dare the impossible. But not without cost.' We do not like to dwell on the cost, even when we mourn those who are lost. We can speak of it, but not what it means.

Writing after the deaths of three young friends in Canada, mountaineer Francis Sanzaro mused, 'Dying happens to someone else, until it doesn't.' It led him to question his real motivation for doing dangerous climbs, the relationship between risk and ego:

> I can tell you that standing on a dime-size foothold with no rope, with your fingertips on a sloping edge, in a remote part of the mountains where one mistake means instant death, in no way translates to a heightened experience. I've been there. You're proud and exhilarated you lived through it and kept it together when most people on the planet couldn't.

> It can change you permanently, not always for the better. But I've had more profound mystical experiences at the park watching my kids play.

Half in love with ourselves, half in love with oblivion. Both elements might seem profoundly selfish to an outside observer. Nearly all mountaineers will say they are aware of the risks they take. In one sense, they're being honest. They have a lot of friends who have died, have probably had near-misses. But the awareness can still remain abstract, almost conceptual. Death is part of the language of mountaineering. A feature can be called a 'death block,' a section a 'death pitch,' or a camp a 'death bivouac'. Perhaps we think that by using death's name we take away some of its threat, some of its power.

Back in the hospital, I shut my book. I closed my eyes and remembered the last time I went soloing. It is always the same memory. It's autumn on Stanage. I have reached a place I can't get down from, a ledge, triangular and jutting. Above me, a greenish overhang. Below, a move I'm not sure I can reverse, rocks shearing to the ground, then the earth sloping away towards Hathersage. To my right, an arête I can't see around. But this ledge is just enough to perch on, a small patch of safety. So, improbably, I sit down and dangle one leg off the side, nonchalantly. It's a windy day, shouts ripped from the crag and carried away to nowhere. There's nobody on the walkers' path except an old man, leaning heavily on his trekking poles, trudging up from the Popular End car park. He wears a huge red-and-white puffy jacket and the sunlight catches his glasses. I wonder if he's going to ask if I'm OK, perched up here alone. I'm an improbable sight: I'm wearing black denim dungaree shorts and a striped T-shirt with my rock shoes, my white-blonde hair tied back with a silk scarf. He notices me and nods. I'm already practising my nonchalant answer: 'Glorious day for it!' In soloing, there are always points of no return. You always meet one eventually. Going up seems exposing, precarious, no rope to catch you if you slip. But reversing is impossible, awkward, perhaps even more dangerous. In the end, you always have to go up.

That's what motherhood feels like. There is no way to undo the sequence of moves that have led to this point, this small blue room, this breathing being who is separate from me, alone in the world, his chest rising and falling under an artificial sun. I cannot drain the yellowness from his body. I cannot stop my own body bleeding. I imagine rewinding through the whole thing, Alfie crawling back into the safety of my womb, becoming smaller and smaller until he is a dot, a pomegranate seed, then the sex that made him in reverse, until I am back, clinging to my partner, burying my head in his chest, dizzy with scent and want. If it is necessary to make death an abstraction as a mountaineer, perhaps it is necessary for a mother to accept death as a constant, concrete possibility. Part of the vigilance of those early days and weeks comes from a sense that the child is helpless. It is no longer enough for you to just live, nourish it through your being, feed it with your pregnant body. You must analyse risk, become instinctive. I thought often of Alison in those days, her level-headed skill in the hills, her way of appraising things, her open, round face, childlike but knowing. She once told a journalist, 'I don't fall. When I rock-climb, I don't fall off. You climb better soloing because you have to. You have to control the fear.' There is an intensity of focus with soloing that is difficult to access in any other way, a complete absorption. You are alone, relying only on your body and your mind, facing the rock and the sequence of moves it demands from you. You must move decisively, quickly, with confidence. But controlling fear is not instinctive.

The days we spent in the hospital have a blue tinge even in my memory. Everything was unnatural. Through the night, I was visited by nurses who would take Alfie's temperature and check the towels he lay on. The visits were called observations and I felt observed too: my uncombed, greasy hair and bleary eyes, my body still sagging from birth, my blood on the sheets of the narrow bed. At mealtimes, I had to queue with the children. Parents aren't allowed food on the Nightingale Ward, but as a breastfeeding mother, I was an exception, sustaining my child. I felt embarrassed, oversized. I tucked into macaroni cheese and watery green beans, smiley potato faces, jelly and ice cream. I thought about school dinners, days suffused with the comfort of someone else being in charge. I was always hungry in hospital, always alert. I was mostly alone, occasional visits from my parents who hovered by the bed, not sure where to look or what to do with their hands. Jess was back in Sheffield, looking after his 12-year-old daughter. I felt abandoned by them, hated myself for feeling it. He had no choice. His ex was away, out of town with their eldest son. In the late stages of pregnancy, I had found myself writing her anguished emails, begging her to go at a different time. I poured out my heart because I had nothing to lose, telling her how terrified I was about having a child. She was kind. But her reassurances made me slam my laptop shut: *I remember the first weeks with a newborn as bliss.* I felt like the wrong kind of woman. I should be like her, blooming into motherhood, suffused with calm. Instead, I was the sort of mother who feared being alone with her child, who could not sleep, could not rest beside him. A blue-lit mother, spectral and haunted, weak with hunger, dreaming of cold hospital toast and jam in plastic sachets. I was soloing.

I was also foggy with sleep deprivation. A nurse patted me kindly on the shoulder. 'You must rest. If you're too tired, it's bad for your milk production.' I felt like a machine, my purpose to respond to Alfie's weak cries. Even his voice began to seem blue, visible, a spool of thread, a blue yarn, unravelling. They call it the baby blues, the time after your milk comes in when love feels overwhelming and tears boil under the surface of your skin. My world was indigo, inside and out. In the hospital, I cried when I took Alfie from his incubator and

I cried when I put him back. I cried when his tiny foot kicked through the air vent. I cried when he yawned and when he sighed. I imagined that I was made of soft things: my mother's denim jeans, the woods near Grindleford, bursting with bluebells in May, the artificial blue of a heated swimming pool, the blue of my dad's eyes, his favourite navy T-shirts. But my blue was more like the tinge of cold, blue lips and fingers, spectral blue. I thought of Maggie Nelson's *Bluets*, in which she describes the approach of death as the swell of a blue wave, a towering wall of sea, a strangely calming sensation:

> To take a breath of water: does the thought panic or excite you? If you are in love with red then you slit or shoot. If you are in love with blue you fill your pouch with stones good for sucking and head down to the river. Any river will do.

On the third or fourth blue day – I forget which, time began to seep – Jess and his daughter came to see us. She sang to him, tender and soft, her voice soothing him as he lay in the tank. While they watched over Alfie, I left the ward, legs shaking, went to get a sandwich and a coffee. I had forgotten daylight, the full spectrum of colour. When I stepped out into the open air, it was like finding a plateau in the hills, or cresting a mountain ridge. It was like a September day in East Greenland when I clambered over rock spires after hours of trudging through glaciers. Just to get into the mountains above the Knud Rasmussen Glacier we'd had to walk for days, weaving in and out to cross huge crevasses, ice on either side threatening to swallow us whole. I found the blue depths of the moulins humbling, the sound of water rushing below. Looking at their intense cyan moved me to tears. But to climb at last was exhilarating, cradled by sun, accepted by gneiss. We had planned to push on for the summit, but we were exhausted from days of trekking. Suddenly, the openness that the ridge gave us – the fjords below like solder, the spires of endless peaks rising to meet the sky – was everything. We danced along it, sat down on a flat ledge. We did not need to go any further. In the hospital, I had escaped my blue confinement. The corridors were beige and featureless. I passed families lost in their private, all-consuming dramas. Windows let the weak winter light through. The cafe was a clamour of uniforms and men clutching flowers. I savoured each colour, the gold tips of the waitress's dip-dyed hair, the silver of the badge on her uniform. Too soon, I had to go back to my blue room and the blue cave of the days.

At Stanage, Andrew is approaching the wooden stile, the last metres back to the car park. His helmet is strapped to the back of his bag, painted like the Scottish flag, royal blue with a white cross. I hang back for a minute. Even now, vivid blue sometimes chokes me, surprises me with its vehemence, its tenacity. I am sobbing again, my body swaying. 'Sorry,' I say. 'I'm just having a moment.' Andrew nods and keeps going.

I know he won't try to diminish my fears. He understands that risk is tangible. Last year on a ski trip, he broke his leg and had to be taken to hospital, agonised. When he still lived in Edinburgh, he fell in love with winter climbing, the brute force of axes and the precarity of crampons. Ice is always a dangerous obsession. Like me, he's lost control of cars on January roads, felt the lightness of steering.

Then there was a climber he never got to meet. Let's call him Adam. For days they had been corresponding online through a climbing forum, planning a winter day out in the hills. Like many, Andrew sometimes enjoys the anonymity of climbing with strangers, meeting people through chat rooms and partnering them in the hills. There is a transactional simplicity to it. Adam was an avatar, a store of knowledge, a name onscreen. Only when they set off into the hills would he become human, a confidant and friend. Let's say the night before they were due to meet was grey and innocuous, headlights shining on damp streets in the city. Let's say Andrew went to the Cumberland after work, nursed a pint of Schiehallion. The landlord had lit the fire, a pug was sunning itself in front of it, rolling on the floorboards. He checked the mountain weather forecast, trawled through the avalanche advice. Perhaps something in him felt heavy, muscles aching from a session at the indoor wall, eyes wearied from the week and his desk. It was a mixed forecast, unstable snow conditions in places.

Avalanches remind us that snow is a liar. It looks vast and monotone, but its layers can lose their grip on one another, the surface hiding fractures. Andrew was used to digging out a square to examine the snow pack. Sometimes, you don't get that far. He closed his eyes. Snowfall. Static. In his flat, he couldn't concentrate on the telly. He texted Adam. *Sorry, change of plan. I don't think it's looking good for tomorrow.* There was a pause before the reply. He crawled under the duvet, snow-coloured. He drifted into a heavy sleep, New Town revellers chorusing outside. In the morning, everything felt muffled. He was buried in sleep, thick, heavy drifts of it. He knew he was still dreaming but he couldn't quite haul himself out. Five am. Nowhere near time to get up. Across the city, Adam was checking his rucksack and loading the boot. He drove with the heating on full blast and the radio soft. When he parked up and set out into the silent hills, he took a picture. *Solo adventures!* The sky and the snow were the same colour, as if the whole landscape was closing around him. There were no birds. He moved through the dawn and he was never seen again. Andrew has mourned this man he never met ever since, convincing himself that he could have saved him. Underneath his guilt, I've always imagined there's something darker, a sense that his instinct saved him, that there could have been two of them lost that day.

I am taking liberties with a story that isn't mine to tell. I know the bare facts and I am filling in gaps, imagining the times in between, the fears and snap decisions. This in itself is unforgivable: I have no right to narrate this, embellish it, just as I have no real right to delve into Alison Hargreaves's innermost life. But if there is no risk in my writing, no fear, there is no pleasure. I have to make myself feel uncomfortable, take chances in the way a mountaineer does, calculating and recalculating, pitching their frail body against the wind. In risk, we feel most alive. A near-miss floods the bloodstream with adrenaline, makes us giddy with relief. I remember a route called Chalkstorm in the Roaches near Staffordshire, a grey muggy day with Andrew. Chalkstorm was a blank slab, hardly a single visible hold on it, tiny pebbles and indents for hands and feet. Leading it made me feel like Spider-Man, scrambling up the improbable, using friction and faith. I once saw a video of legendary climber Johnny Dawes completing it without using his hands, teetering on the sheerness, driving with his legs. Chalkstorm was tense and nervy, my feet slipping from underneath me without warning, a dozen moves that I had to brace every muscle for. It was smooth and endless. It reminded me of a blank page, the sense of possibility, the fear of humiliation.

As a writer and as a climber, I like to walk the line between safety and terror, living in a constant sense of unease or gratitude, anxiety then happiness. Blank pages and blank slabs are where I write myself, the trace like an ECG trace. They are spaces where I face my fears. But in motherhood, the line of tolerable fear is altered, becomes a threat. The ground becomes a safe place, the sky threatening. There is familiarity in the horizontal, relief in beds and cots and lying side by side, and instinct tells us to cling to it. To climb as a new mother is not the same rush of exhilaration it once was. It is dangerous to leave the ground, the blue sky waiting, the blue of distance beyond. And perhaps in this distance I recognise something I should know already from my writing: it's not just my own life I toy with.

/\/\/\/\ SECOND PITCH

When she reaches your belay stance, she is out of breath and you exchange few words. What she says is soon taken by the wind anyway, lifted somewhere just out of your grasp. You take back the gear you'll need for the next pitch, sort it and clip it neatly in place. You have always had systems. Gold cam next to green cam. Quickdraws at the back. Slings looped into knots and secured with karabiners. You're sure you could find them all with your eyes shut.

From a distance, you are not proud sentinels. Your bodies are not flags. You are just two shadows on the rock's tired face, two bruises, two bags under its eyes. You both smudge and blur at the edges. You are all watercolour today, your outlines bleeding into the face. You like it that way. You want to be inconspicuous. That's why you love climbing slabs so much, the way the angle forces you to lean towards the surface of the rock as if you're trying to be part of it. Balance and breath. Overhangs are all showmanship and power, hauling yourself backwards, levering yourself into space. Slabs are intimate.

So much of climbing is this: the moments in between, rummaging for the right equipment, gathering in rope and paying it out, waiting to begin again. This is the real work, the tedium of preparation and the sunken aftermath, earning the right to start over, the right to trespass on rock. You have learned to love it, to see these moments as existing out of time. It is a version of what the landscape does, slow renewal, covering inflicted tracks, growing over what is cut down and shifting into new placements, new shapes. The earth forgetting its intruders. Let me be slow as that, you think, let me take my time.

You vow to savour the minutes before setting off, the enforced stillness, looking up at the route. It is rehearsal and performance all at once. You place your hand on her shoulder and pat firmly. It is a forced gesture, awkward, but she smiles up at you then goes back to sorting out the stitch plate and the ropes, getting ready to belay again. This is how you work best, heads down, unspeaking, sharing a common purpose. A tractor starts up below, struggling to life, and a collie begins to round up sheep, turning the flock into neat triangles and arrows, streamlined movement. Your rest is over.

'On belay,' she says, and you must begin again.

CLIMBING THE WALLS

2019

The land near Strines is flat and brooding, as if the moors draped the sky over them like a second-hand blanket and huddled beneath, finding no comfort. To me, it's always been foreboding, a no man's land between Sheffield and Cheshire, rust-flecked ground and slopes that pull your body down towards bracken and steely reservoirs. When the heather grows violet, it seems bruised and swollen, pummelled by life. The narrow lanes and scant trees are held in my rear-view mirror now as I drive with Alfie. He's cosy in a knitted white cardigan, dozing in his car seat. Dawn is loud with birdsong, misty and mild. I don't pass any other traffic. I drive with my heart hammering and my limbs tingling, my movements slow and deliberate. Alfie sighs and stirs, uncurls his hands. He is barely six months old, swamped by the moorland around him, delicate inside my dirty, neglected car. I am afraid of him waking up, the siren of his cry. I am afraid of everything.

Yesterday, we packed Jess's van – a battered left-hand-drive Karmann camper with a red, womb-like interior – with wellies, jumpers, red wine and tins of food and set off into Derbyshire towards a tiny music festival, organised by friends. I followed in my own car. I could see my stepson and stepdaughter in the van's rear window, clutching a portable speaker, throwing shapes and pulling faces at each other. It was threatening rain when our convoy reached the turn-off to Strines. I recognised the narrow lanes and open fields from days spent climbing Derwent Edge, looking out for hares in the undergrowth and marvelling at the almost perfect circular holes in the rock. It's said you can even spot white hares out here. They have assumed mythic significance, too pale for a world that has slowly melted around them, obvious prey for birds. Once or twice I thought I glimpsed a brown hare, impossibly long and lithe, bounding from grass to rock, wide eyes and strong haunches. Nearing the festival, I should have been in my element, the landscape of old adventures, fell runs up from Ladybower where I stepped on patches of shifting ground, the whole bog seeming to move under me. But I was tense and irritable, labouring under a fog of fatigue. The Derwent Valley hemmed me in.

When we got close, the festival winked with fairy lights. It was small and contained: one large gazebo, a fire pit and a few pleasantly dishevelled tents perched on a mound of grass. On a hill facing it, caravans and tents were huddled together. This was the brainchild of a local cafe owner, an ex-musician, effortlessly cool. We set up our camp chairs and cooked hotdogs and canned chilli, fed Alfie purée from a packet and blueberry yoghurt. There is a photo of him from that afternoon, held in the crook of his elder brother's arm. My stepson's hair is a sandy mane, lifted by the wind, Alfie is quizzical and rosy-cheeked. They both wear a half-smile. We put Alfie down to sleep in his Moses basket in the camper and he gurgled happily. I settled him with a breastfeed, holding him close and making the lights as soft as possible, singing to him gently.

Since he started on purées and solid foods, he had been dropping his milk feeds, favouring breadsticks, yoghurt and pears. I'd been feeding him less and less. It was dark outside and the lights on the hill should have seemed benign and comforting. I sat at a fold-out table drinking wine with Jess, then we took it in turns to wander around the festival, straying close to the fire and its wall of heat. I greeted friends, nodded my head half-heartedly in time to the band, admired the wild, buoyant energy of the drummer. She had a rope of long dark hair over her shoulder. I had the urge to grab it with both my hands and hold on for dear life. I remembered a story of my gran when she was a sinewy child, grabbing the pigtails of an older girl who had been bullying her brother and swinging from them until the girl howled in agony. My gran, who put a brick through the Salvation Army window for fun, chased her brother round the house with a pickaxe and swung it at his bedroom door. They had been fighting over the last piece of cheese. I come from a long line of tough women. In the early days of motherhood, I often imagined they would be ashamed of me, of the heavy weather I made of things.

I was tense. The firelight across the faces of people I knew from Sheffield made them seem devilish. Their dancing was macabre, bacchanalian, debauched. A man with a goatee loomed towards me, singing, and I flinched.

A drunk woman in a rainbow coat had draped herself over a hay bale. Scurrying back through the darkness, I hid outside the van with a hoodie wrapped around my shoulders, talking to my friend Helen and her partner, Deb, struggling to concentrate on what they were saying. Jess and his son took off into the noisy heart of the festival, swigging rum from a bottle, rolling with the music. I drank hot tea, then water. My mouth always seemed to be parched. Alfie was sleeping through the thumping beats, strangely lulled by his new surroundings. I thought curling up next to him would comfort me, but in the night, I felt the walls of the camper van collapsing under me and crushing both of us. It's what I've always imagined rockfall would feel like, or an avalanche. We were suffocating. I rocked backwards and forwards, holding my knees. Jess rolled in late, smelling of spirits and cigarette smoke. When he tried to touch me, I sobbed with anger. I wanted to get out of the van, wanted to drive into the night with my child, to be alone with him. As soon as it was light, I would go.

Now, driving back towards Sheffield's outskirts, I am gripped by the urge to detour. I need edges and stone, something I can stand on the brink of. I need to sense the limits of Derbyshire, places where the land swoops away from me. I drive past Stanage and the gritstone outcrops closest to home. By Burbage Brook I park the car, leave Alfie sleeping in the back and sit on the bonnet, looking out across the grey teeth of the edge. Even my gaze is strained. There is nobody else here. The path is tan-coloured and inviting, dipping towards the Fox House pub. Trees cling to the rocks and improbably survive, ash trees mostly. I scan the edge for routes I once climbed. But I cannot see them. Everything vertical is indistinct. My phone buzzes in my pocket. It's Jess.

'Where are you?' he asks groggily.

'I'm at the rocks. The place . . . the place I used to climb. The rocks near home.'

This familiar landscape has become suddenly nameless, inaccessible to me. Ever since I was a child, I've been in love with Peak District geography, pored over maps and route guides, relishing the specificity of edges and hills, climbing routes and rivers. Carl Wark. Froggatt and Curbar. Higgar Tor. Sunset Slab and Ellis's Eliminate. Suddenly, my private landscape has gaps in it.

'Jess, why can't I remember the name?' I am panicking again, my voice high and thin.

'It's OK. Everything's going to be OK. I'm coming home. I'll meet you there.'

I do not know where I am. I can go through the motions of walking, moving, following the road. But my topography is altered, warped. I get back behind the wheel and numbly drive. There are dog walkers on the streets of Nether Edge, runners in fluorescent jackets setting off for the long drag up towards Lady Cannings Plantation and the Norfolk Arms. The houses still have curtains drawn, soft and private. I unlock our front door and hoist Alfie inside in his car seat. Then I set him down at the bottom of the stairs, sit on a step halfway up and facing him and let sobs overtake my body, huge, gulping underwater sobs. Alfie does not cry. He just scans me intently with his beady eyes, never lets his stare leave me. He knows everything about me already and he is only six months old.

As a runner and climber, I've often seen the landscape of my body as an outcrop, sturdy and self-contained. I like feeling solid. Descriptions of female climbers tend to emphasise their surprising strength, the contrast between femininity and physical power. Jim Ballard boasted of

Alison that one of the best climbers in the world was 5 foot 4 and a size 10 in a dress. As a young woman, she was slim and boyish, her strength concentrated in her small frame. My image of her as a mountaineer is of a strong woman alone, intent and hunched over her ice axes, or levering her way up a gritstone overhang with the wind blowing through her bark-coloured hair, skin glowing from exertion. When I think of myself outdoors, I am solitary too, running to the top of Blencathra, stooped and serious, or climbing a hill alone in rain, a book stowed in my backpack. I like to sprint along Burbage when there's nobody else around. I like to feel the edges of myself. In many ways, I have aspired to the condition of gritstone, proud and weathered, constant. But motherhood changes the body's landscape, introduces a fundamental duality. Breastfeeding Alfie was the most intimate experience of my life, perhaps even more than birthing him. We were attached to one another. He cleaved to me and I held him tight.

During pregnancy, I did not believe that my flat breasts could nurture a child. The thought made me incredulous. Since I lost weight as a teenager, my shape had always been elongated, sharpened by miles of mountain running.

Friends joked about my boyish figure, my inability to wear strapless dresses. In the days when I waited for Alfie to arrive, I squeezed around my nipples, desperate to see pearly drops of colostrum glistening there, proof that I could produce milk. In my rational brain, I knew that breast size has nothing to do with the ability to breastfeed, but – not for the first time – my A-cup bra size became a focus for my anxiety. When Alfie was born and my milk came, I barely recognised myself, swelling and taut with liquid, desperate for him to drain the new fullness of my breasts.

The first few days of feeding are gruelling and sore, a struggle to get the baby to latch on, to swallow enough goodness. Colostrum is thick and golden, a nectar that the newborn only needs in tiny amounts, a teaspoonful at each feed. Like all babies, Alfie was constantly hungry, constantly suckling. I don't remember how I first helped him latch on to me, but I do remember his ardent, determined drinking, how I cradled the softness of his neck and head, learned how to hold him under my arm like a rugby ball. I remember the ritual of guiding him to my nipples. Two days after he was born, I was flooded with milk. It came with a choking sorrow, a sense of overwhelming love and responsibility. I produced milk and let out tears. I learned about foremilk and rich hindmilk, the way Alfie's cry and the sight of his scrunched face triggered the 'let-down reflex'. The involuntary nature of this was unnerving, milk leaking through my bra and top, my clothes smelling sour. I was no longer an outcrop, a clutch of rock. I was a waterfall, a stream, and he was wading through me, paddling in me, thirsty and keen. My body was no longer a climber's. It was fluid, soft. He was nearly always attached to me.

In those early months, Alfie's appetite made it difficult to be away from him. If I missed a feed, I got mastitis – milk fever – and my breasts hardened with lumps, a fever breaking on my brow. It felt like a rebuke for my independence. Alison Hargreaves struggled to be separate from Tom when he was small too, even when she began to crave physical independence. She could only manage short, efficient bursts of activity in the Peak District, soloing or running to rebuild her strength. With my own child, I often thought of her and wondered if she'd found it intrusive. Feeding Alfie alone at night flooded me with calm, a pale, silky kind of joy: his bread-rich scent, his warmth, the small noises as he sucked. But so often breastfeeding felt invasive too, his rooting and tugging, moments in public when I struggled to latch him on, turning my body away and fumbling with buttons. When he was just weeks old, we took him to a friend's Christmas party and I spent four hours in the corner with my top unbuttoned and my face flushed, trying to maintain conversation with the people around me, all gaudy jumpers and tissue-paper crowns. I was wearing a powder-blue jumpsuit, but it was mostly open. I felt fleshy, overripe.

Part of me knew I shouldn't be embarrassed about my breasts, ashamed of this natural, ancient process, but another part wanted to run for cover, to carry Alfie out to Stanage Edge and crawl into the mouth of Robin Hood's Cave, hunker down with him in green silence and darkness, form a new privacy, just the two of us. I hated strangers glimpsing my body. And sometimes I hated his pure need and the way it summoned me. Even the word 'engorged' made me feel nauseous. I disliked the feeling of strain, the hardness of my breasts when they were full, the relief when I fed him. My body did not feel like mine. It was not the craggy vista I had grown up with. If Alison shared my ambivalence about breastfeeding, she never wrote of it. But it comforted me to think of her longing for freedom and slimness, to be able to wedge her body into an off-width crack in the rocks again and shimmy upwards towards the light.

Whenever Alison was separated from the hills, she pined for open land and big skies. Ever since she was a teenager, she'd found confidence in precarious situations, testing her limits on mountain routes, seeing freedom in high places where others might just have seen hardship and risk. In 1977 at Stanage, another climber on a close-by route fell and tangled in Alison's ropes, peeling her from the rock. She hit the ground and broke both bones in her lower left leg. Consigned to inactivity and crutches for months, she lost her sense of identity, writing in her diary: 'Feel short-tempered at the moment. Oh, a woman is so missing snow, ice, rock.'

There's something strangely formal, strangely detached about Alison's early tendency to refer to herself in the third person in her journals. It's as if she was always watching herself from afar, peering down at her own body from the top of the crag above her, or gazing up in adulation from the ground. As if she lacked the self-confidence to use the assertiveness of 'I'. She spent her confinement poring over climbing guides and as soon as she could walk unaided, went to Black Rocks in Cromford to climb a route called Railway Slab. Even if she couldn't lead, she was delighted to be out on rock again, reacquainting herself with its shapes, the curious physical demands it makes.

The months after giving birth are a kind of convalescence and every new mother has to care for their altered body. As someone used to endurance, to strength, to my limbs doing my bidding, I struggled to come to terms with my weak muscles, the loose skin on my stomach, the blood from my stitches, my new and tender breasts. I did not identify with these things. They were not part of me. I did not feel like the same woman who'd slept on a glacier in East Greenland or danced my way up routes in a Welsh slate quarry. Two weeks after giving birth, I tried to jog, haltingly through the woods at Brincliffe Edge. I felt as if everything in my body was dragging, pulled towards my feet. My limbs were strangely elastic, loosened by the hormones released in breastfeeding. I couldn't go far before I felt the twinge of milk arriving again. All of my energy was bunched in Alfie, his tiny, strong limbs, his strident voice and knowing eyes. It was as if I had given birth to the best part of me. I paraded him in woollen booties and yellow babygros, dragging the shell of my body round after us.

Like me, Alison was shocked by the demands of her newborn, the disturbed nights of feeding and changing Tom, soothing him when he had wind. She hadn't joined any antenatal groups and knew no other mothers with babies the same age, still less any climbers who might understand her sudden claustrophobia. Meerbrook Lea, the house she lived in with Jim, was splendidly isolated. In the early months with her son, that isolation must have lost something of its splendour, her husband working long hours to try and bail out his failing climbing shop business, domestic tensions running high.

Alison contented herself with walks with her retired parents, reliving the adventures she'd been on as a child, taking Tom on trips to Snowdonia. Like me, she found the physical bond between her and her son in those early days a source of both profound joy and mild frustration. Though she often longed to be outdoors, Alison found happiness in watching Tom explore the world, sitting with him for hour after hour, delighted by his tiny discoveries. Time with a young baby is both fascinating and boring, a wonder and a chore. This is no contradiction. Motherhood splits the mother and creates parallel selves. Throughout those months, part of me ran like a dog off the leash and part of me never let Alfie go for a second. I became 'a woman', the third person Alison created in her diaries, mature and bewildered, naive and profound, always standing apart from myself.

For Alison, as for me, happiness was inextricably linked to landscape, to mountains and the freedom to go to them, move through them, test herself against their slopes. Though she adored Tom, she still had climbing ambitions and, in the process of slowly getting her fitness back in Derbyshire, she found a renewed sense of purpose. She always said that to be a good mother, she needed to be happy. And she could only be happy if she climbed. When Tom was almost one, she took her first trip away from home, back to her familiar stomping ground in the Alps. With her climbing partner (Steve Aisthorpe again, the same climber who was with her when she was pregnant on the Eiger), she battled for days up the face of Les Droites, tackling nearly 4,000 metres of steep ice, vertical rock and abseiling back down from the summit in ominous clouds. She became the first

British woman to have climbed it. But the exposure of tackling a big route after so long made her feel vulnerable. Alison arrived home just in time for Tom's first birthday and was soon up to her elbows in flour, making her boy a huge mushroom-shaped cake. I can picture her movements, almost frantic.

At home, she was afraid of being trapped. In the mountains, the space around her was daunting, the air colder and the sky wilder than she remembered. Each state was tinged with the memory of its opposite.

When Alfie was five months old, he began to steal food from our plates. He loved the ooze of strawberries and the crunch of watermelon. He spooned purée clumsily towards his mouth, took handfuls of porridge from my bowl in the mornings. As his appetite for bread and cheese and broccoli grew, I began to dream of weaning him, of reclaiming some of the boundaries of my body, demarcating its edges again. Bottles of formula began to replace night feeds. My breasts lost their new-found plumpness. My muscles began to feel stronger and running was no longer painful. On a trip to Scotland, I took off into the Ardnamurchan hills in a downpour with my parents' dog, not minding that I was drenched, the scent of wet ponies sharpening the air.

For months, I had secretly thought of stopping breast-feeding, the new thrill of Jess giving Alfie a bottle, holding him tight while he guzzled like a piglet or lamb. I would not be tied to the house, the routine of feeds replaced with breakfast, lunch and dinner. I felt a twinge of guilt when I read about Jasmin Paris, the ultra-runner who paused during the 268-mile Montane Spine Race to pump breastmilk for her toddler and still went on to win the competition. She set a new record for the race, stopping at each checkpoint to express milk. There are many stories of breastfeeding as heroism, women who struggled to establish feeding but managed it against the odds, mums who made sacrifices to keep breastfeeding when back at work. My experience had been easy, my desire to stop largely selfish. But it seemed Alfie was leading me too, showing less and less interest in breastmilk.

For a while, I continued to breastfeed before bed, cradling Alfie on the sofa at night to the sounds of instrumental lullabies. But he was impatient and fractious, turning his head away and rubbing his eyes. I knew my milk supply was drying up. Those last feeds became a fog of tenderness. I was gripped by the urge to pull Alfie close and smell him, bury myself in his sparse hair, hold his pudgy fingers. After months of longing for independence, I was suddenly unable to put him down in his cot. Holding him to my breast brought a surge of contentment, a blanket-soft feeling.

This was when I first started to lose my geography. It was subtle at first. Alone in my own bed, I found myself cuddling his little maroon snowsuit with a fur trim, sleeping with it held to my chest, then waking in a cold sweat, convinced the suit was his lifeless body. I clutched it and imagined him older in the snow, pictured him toddling through all the white-covered quiet places of the city, the parks suddenly nameless to me. I thought of his footprints in the woods by the side of the stream. There were crossing places, rough stones that dogs scampered over, low overhanging branches. There was a memorial to a plane that came down here decades ago, crashing into the bank. There were climbing frames and swings where children squealed to be pushed higher. There were places for sliding, families dragging sledges obediently up the slopes. How could I keep Alfie safe and near if I did not know where he was walking? By day, I became irritable. I was free to go climbing, take stretches of time for myself, but more and more I wanted the comfort of Alfie's body, the good heat of him.

One day, a health visitor called round while I was unloading bags of groceries from the car.

'Is this a good time?'

We drank lukewarm tea from mugs decorated with pictures of biscuits. The health visitor's said I KNOW HOW TO PARTY underneath a drawing of a pink frosted party ring. She asked about the crying spells: how long they lasted, whether I was getting enough sleep. She did not ask about the place names and their slow vanishing.

She left me with the details of an Australian website offering cognitive behavioural therapy. A gym for moods. You had to pay. Then you had to answer a series of 'initial questions'. I scrolled through them on my phone at night but none of them seemed relevant. The only important question now was *Where am I?*

I searched the internet for advice:

You should stop gradually.

You should stop quickly if you're going to do it. Like pulling off a plaster.

It's just hormones.
It's sleep deprivation.
You're grieving for your child.

I pored over articles: 'The Hardest Eight Weeks of My Life' and 'What Nobody Told Me About Oxytocin'. I scrolled through National Childbirth Trust guidance on stopping breastfeeding, found only support to continue. *Do you really need to stop?* The World Health Organization recommends breastfeeding until the age of two. But mostly, I read maps the way I used to as a child, running my finger from left to right and from top to bottom, following the course of the A57 out through Broomhill and Crosspool, skirting Rivelin and curving towards open land. I could remember driving out to Ladybower to climb in the quarries, misjudging the bends, looking out for the wire hair of the moors.

I always imagine that Alison experienced the twinges of separation from Tom – physical and mental – as keenly as I did, even as she longed for mountains. This is pure speculation, but it comforts me. Perhaps she felt she was forgetting places too and she needed to go mountaineering to recover them. Her love was intense but her need for solitude was intense too. Motherhood is a state of perpetual instinct, not logical decision-making. It immerses you in the way climbing does, but the calculations feel more uncertain, more perilous and fraught.

When Tom was still a toddler, Alison knew she wanted another child. Her biographers write of alleged tensions between her and Jim, arguments that had begun when she was just 20, the differences between them becoming more and more apparent. With him running the business, she was expected to tend the home, and having a child had only exacerbated that structural division. A second would add to the strain. And yet she pined for new motherhood once more. I understand this – when I was at my most exhausted and Alfie was waking multiple times in the night, I'd complain bitterly of tiredness, only to pine for him the moment I set him down and dream about having a newborn again. Adverts on TV with cooing, gurgling babies made me tearful, sentimental. I entertained ideas of trying for a second child, only to reject them the next minute. Alison's need was more persistent, more constant. Her biographers say that she tried to talk Jim round and, when that proved futile, she made her case in a letter to him: 'Dear Jim, I should love to have another baby . . . there are many reasons, some of which I have written down, as you are not prepared to listen to me . . .'

There is something in her cheerful pragmatism that I find endearing, both childish and knowing. And she got her wish. She was pregnant again by July 1990 and gave birth to her daughter Kate in 1991. By then, Alison's biographers note that Jim's business was in severe trouble, close to bankruptcy. Even their home at Meerbrook Lea was under threat. And there were two children to nurture. The reality of punishing routines and low energy. The months that followed were fractured, sleepless, punctured by self-doubt. Alison began to regard herself as a failed climber, a failed wife and a failed mother. She felt she had achieved nothing since Tom was born. On 5 June 1991, she wrote:

> Whatever happened to that young, self-confident 'I can do it' teenager? I now seem to be able to 'turn away' from anything and take the easiest

> option . . . I think I do my best – it's obviously not good enough.

She always compared herself brutally to her contemporaries, climbers like Catherine Destivelle from France whose adventures were often plastered across the pages of magazines, glamorously framed. Catherine was an acquaintance of Alison, a Parisian who had learned to climb young at Forêt de Fontainebleau on the outskirts of the city. She was a star of the international competition circuit, an icon among climbers. Alison stared enviously at Catherine's pin-up smile and cropped dark hair, the power in her tanned, lithe limbs. Once again, she found distraction and solace in Peak District soloing, at Birchen Edge and Burbage North and Ramshaw Rocks, ticking off solo routes in her battered guidebook. She once described solo climbing as:

> totally opposite to looking after the kids because it's so self-indulgent. When you're with kids they demand, demand, demand, demand and there's no give, give, give. And of course solo climbing is totally self-indulgent. You do what you want to do.

It also offered her an escape from the gloomy realities of a national recession and Jim's failing business. On rock, she could feel self-sufficient and capable. For a brief window of time, she only needed to worry about pleasing herself, pushing her body and testing her nerve, climbing until the light failed her. Mountaineering was the only career she could imagine.

Climbing was Alison's passion, but now her climbing decisions were being influenced by practicality, by raw need. In 1992, she hatched a bold plan to return to the Alps and attempt a solo winter ascent of the Matterhorn's north face, a feat never achieved by a woman. It was February, the ski resorts lonely, the snow engulfing. With no money, Alison could barely afford to eat in the local bars of Chamonix and Zermatt. And though she relished waking up in the hulking shadow of the Mont Blanc range, she became tearful when she saw other people's children. She knew Kate and Tom would have enjoyed coming with her, scampering in the snow, but it would have made it more difficult to concentrate.

In 1992, Alison set out from the Hörnli Alpine hut by starlight on a cold, still morning. Her crampons on the icefield were testing, searching. She waited for the ground to answer her. But she was met with brittle, dirty ice, impossible to stand on securely, ice axes skittering off the surface. After detouring to an easier route, she had to rescue a party of men in difficulty: they were high on the mountain with inadequate equipment, ropes too short to abseil with. In the gruelling descent with them, she got frostbite. Her plans for the Matterhorn abandoned, she lay in a Chamonix hospital bed and heard that Catherine Destivelle had soloed the north face of the Eiger. Alison had narrowly escaped needing amputation.

In his book *Starlight and Storm*, climber Gaston Rébuffat says that in mountains we are 'surrounded by the silence of forgetfulness'. But that silence is hard won. For Alison, the world of mountaineering had become fraught even while the act of climbing remained joyful, all-consuming. Rébuffat established his reputation as the first man to climb all six of the legendary great north faces of the Alps – the Grandes Jorasses, the Piz Badile, the Petit Dru, the Matterhorn, the Cima Grande di Lavaredo, and the Eiger. After her failed Alpine trip, Alison began to plan a repeat of his classic climbs, the toughest, grandest routes in the Alps, laced with romance and danger. She would climb them solo, something never attempted before by a woman. Jim assumed the role of chief carer for the children and the family travelled in convoy round Europe, chasing good weather and Alison's ambitions, camping wherever they could, often soaked and muddy, cold, hungry and tired. The sense of expectation placed on the trip made climbing a pragmatic and sometimes fraught endeavour, replete with all the pressures of a job. Though she eventually succeeded, she had to deviate from her planned route on the Eiger and, on the way to the summit, she found the dead body of another climber, clothes shredded. It was the first time she had seen a corpse.

Shaken and unprepared, she felt the need to stay with him, to crouch beside him. She said later in an interview with Jenni Murray on *Woman's Hour*: 'I just didn't feel that I could leave him there . . . I can't say why. I just felt I owed it to him to get him off the mountain.'

Eventually a helicopter came and took them off together, a rescue party summoned by the dead climber's friend after he hadn't returned. Her description of the incident led Murray to ask whether the stark sighting of a dead body made her think twice about mountaineering with two little ones at home. Alison replied to the question the same way she always tackled questions about risk:

> If I felt what I was doing was so risky then I would actually stop doing it. Everybody has accidents but we have accidents doing everything all day . . . you never know when those risks are going to be . . . I do tend to minimise the risks involved in climbing and that's why I carry on.

Those were the last words of the interview.

/\/\/\/\/\ LAST PITCH

This is the final pitch. You have walked to the right side of the continuation wall and the top of the buttress is less than 20 metres away. It would be an exaggeration to say that the sun is coming out, but the air feels lighter, fresher, less encumbered somehow. One easy pitch. You nod, 'Climbing,' one last time and hoist yourself up, moving leftwards on a series of good holds. You really could do this route in your sleep. As a teenager, you climbed it at night, did it wearing walking boots, always solo. Its simplicity is its freedom, you can sink into your own body, let your skeleton do the work. You move almost with a flourish, exaggerating every step. It is hardly even climbing. You are here because it is a classic, because of her hesitancy, because of the weather, because of the grassy plateaus of the ledges and her tangible fear, her lack of trust in her own frame. You were kind. You did not say it was insulting, that the route was too easy for you. You begin to whistle again.

Then of course the rock punishes you. You've been cocky, swaggering, taking the route for granted. You move your right foot without looking, arms still hanging loosely by your sides, and the sudden glassiness of the rock astonishes you, ambushes you, its glossy sheen and slick. The air animates you. You've not bothered to place gear yet and suddenly you're off, down, ungainly, and she's holding you. You laugh it off, make a sarcastic comment and she barely smiles. Rock turned slippery. Rock turned fickle. Rock angered by overuse, by centuries of boots, grasping hands, niches taken as given, taken as read. There is little in Derbyshire quite as polished as this, quite as popular. Kraken Corner maybe. Routes at the Popular End.

You're back on the ladder again, barely using your feet this time, placing a cam for good measure. Your body is a diagonal, a cut on the rock's cheek. You are under the shallow scoop now, the last move. You relish it. At the top, the wind baffles you, sweeping your hair over your eyes. You laugh to yourself, laugh at yourself, remembering the slip, the dangling humiliation of it. You sling a loop of rope around a rock and shout, 'Safe,' repeating it for good measure. The sky is the colour of whisky. You want to drink it neat.

HOMECOMING

'It takes faith to penetrate the world the way a cormorant must. If I were one I would have to promise myself every day, "The water looks impervious: but at the right moment it will give." I sat in the niche for a long time. I realised I didn't know any more than the last time I sat there. I didn't know anything about anything.'

M. John Harrison, *Climbers*

2019

I have imagined death twice. There was the last hour of Alfie's birth when I thought I was going to die at the surgeon's hand, the moment she brought out sharp instruments and said she was going to cut me and all

I could do was sob, 'I'm scared, I'm scared,' like a mantra. Then there was the quiet afternoon in our bright front room when I was convinced I was going to suffocate, choke on my own breath, collapse inwards like a quarry after an explosion. I had almost fully weaned Alfie and had taken a trip to Hebden Bridge to speak about one of my books at the Trades Club, along with a host of others. Throughout the talks, I welled up for no reason, wrung my hands in my lap. This was nothing new. For weeks I had been inarticulate with tears, angry one moment and self-pitying the next. On the drive back through West Yorkshire into South Yorkshire, past the old mill chimneys and dark stones, I felt strangely flat and heavy. It wasn't a dull day, but the view from my windscreen was pale somehow, washed out. Everything had taken on a bleached colour. It was the opposite of standing on a summit in clear weather where the horizon seems sharpened by blue, each mountain outline standing proud. I could not understand where this whiteness had come from, what the new veil meant.

Everything around me seemed blanched but washed with dirt, like the colour of sheep bones or wool. It was as if I were wearing tinted glasses, whitewashing the fields and houses, the long stretch of our road. When I reached home, I was shaking as if with cold but the weather was fine, mild late summer. I almost pushed past Jess in my desire to see and hold Alfie and crouched beside him as he played on the floor, hardly glancing up at me, busy with his cars and battered wooden blocks. I was tense and irritable, exchanged short words with Jess about something unimportant. I think I had wanted him and Alfie to come with me on the trip to Hebden, but they had needed to stay behind with Jess's daughter, help with homework. One moment I was reaching out a hand to stroke Alfie's cheek, the next I was hunched over on the floor, yelling that I was afraid of him. Every breath was a struggle, my chest tight. I felt like I was back in the birthing suite again, looking at the scalpels. A new grim mantra droned through my head: 'I'm going to die, I'm going to die, I'm going to die.' It seemed inevitable, logical almost, just as it had then. If I could not breathe, how could I live? My heart thudded with a dull ache. The whole room was white, mucky snow, wrong sunlight, damp mist and suffocating cloud. I shook and rattled and my teeth chattered in my chest. Jess held Alfie close and I felt ashamed of myself, as if my own son now needed to be protected from me.

In the aftermath, once the shuddering subsided, I was eerily calm. Mountain weather – the stillness after a storm has wreaked havoc. The paleness had lifted from everything. Later that afternoon, my mum and dad came to see us after an anguished call from Jess. We nursed cold cups of tea and sat close together, not touching. My mother recognised what I'd had as a panic attack. But when I described the drive back from Hebden Bridge, the lost, diminished colours, her face clouded and she seemed unsettled.

'That's exactly how it was for me when I stopped breastfeeding you.'

I knew about my mother's menopausal depression, how it hung over the house when I was a teenager, and she'd talked about her postnatal depression. She'd whispered me the story of the afternoon she'd climbed to the top of a multi-storey car park in Chesterfield with me in her arms, bawling my lungs out, and stood at the lip of the concrete, imagining what it would be like to drop me from the edge. The story almost became a joke over the years, a family legend, an anecdote, a sarcastic rebuke when I misbehaved. But I did not know that the weeks leading up to that moment were suffused with white, the colours of her world drained, as if the milk I had stopped taking was flooding from her and changing everything she could see for miles. It was uncanny, unnerving. I gripped her hand tight, my nails making tiny horseshoes in her palm.

In the days after that, I was afraid for Alfie and for myself. But gradually, I felt my hold on the world growing stronger, my fingers tightening, my muscles flexing. I was no longer afraid I was going to die. Colours were seeping in, watercolour at first, fluid, then oil on canvas. I thought often of my mother, the inherited nature of postnatal depression, postnatal experience. I have never said this to her aloud, but I find the multi-storey car park story frightening. It precedes my memory, but I feel the height in my bones. Part of me is still up there, tiny and raging under the Brutalist roof, facing the sky, the roundabout and roads below, the spire of the market town. When I picture it, I am not in my mother's arms but outside the car park, watching her as she holds me, looks down at the drop. And sometimes I am inside her face, staring out at her tiny child and the distance below. Could an edge like that make a person love the dizziness of height? Does it teach them to cling on tight and climb their way to safety?

*

As I recovered, I charted Alison's recovery from her worst moments of depression, her return to the world of high-profile mountaineering. In it, I found the comfort of movement and the thrilling fear of the multi-storey, my mother's story. It was disconcerting, heartbreaking, made me twitch in my own skin. It was also awe-inspiring. When Alison was at her lowest ebb, she sought redemption, a renewal of faith in her abilities, on the highest mountain in the world. In an interview with Matt Comesky in 1995, when she looked back on her career, Alison linked her desire to climb Everest to childhood ambition and an infatuation with wild, inhospitable, breathtaking places:

> . . . At school I used to look at books on the Antarctic and I always wanted to join the British Antarctic Survey. I couldn't because I'm a girl. But I'm fascinated by snowy places. And, obviously, being brought up in a sort of mountaineering, hill-walking background, Everest was always at the back of my mind.

I couldn't because I'm a girl. As an established climber, she could now take her place anywhere, attempt any climb she liked.

Though busy, brutal and expensive, a mountaineering cliché, a playground of the rich, Everest still holds a lure, especially for someone wanting to approach it 'pure', without the help of porters or bottled oxygen. Perhaps it is the legend, the pressing sense of history. Or the remarkable vantagepoint it offers, or the challenge itself, the indescribable pull of standing on the roof of the world, a point which gets higher every year. At the time when Alison was compelled by it, it was not what it is now, an illustration of global conflict, site of economic inequality where rich amateurs join ad-hoc expeditions to make yet another ascent of the world's highest peak. When Alison first attempted Everest in 1994, with her family waiting at base camp, she reached a point just 300 metres short of the summit. Defeat must have been crushing, the bone-tired return to the tents. But she was soon given the opportunity to return, to try to climb it from Tibet, on the north side. Despite the financial difficulties of getting herself on another expedition, she went. This time, the kids stayed at home.

Some medical experts had assumed that climbing Everest without bottled oxygen was suicidal – until 1978, when Reinhold Messner and Peter Habeler did it. Alison joined their ranks with her astonishing climb in May 1995, reaching the summit unsupported, with no help carrying her equipment. She was overcome with emotion. She dedicated the feat to her children, radioing them from the summit to tell them how much she adored them. Perhaps she loved them even more in that moment because she was on top of the world. She was in a fellowship of mountaineers who admired her. She was as far from her troubled marriage and responsibilities as it was possible to be, looking down on her life from above, marvelling at its strangeness and complexity.

Her feat led Messner to describe her as 'the greatest alpinist ever as a woman' (always the caveat). Alison arrived back in England to a media frenzy, a flurry of interviews and offers, questions, adulation and doubt – her achievements were praised, almost universally. She was described as a 'plucky mum of two' and 'Alison of Everest'. It was acknowledged as 'one of the greatest climbs in history'. The attention was uncomfortable and exhausting. She longed for Rébuffat's 'silence of forgetfulness' again. And there was only one place to find it.

In his poem 'The Last Swim', Michael Laskey writes:

> September, October . . . one thing
> you don't know at the time is when
> you've had your last swim: the weather
> may hold, may keep nudging you in.

He's writing about the seasons, but I've never been able to get his words out of my mind because they sound a sombre note in me, chill me with the certainty of implication:

> Only afterwards, sometimes days on,
> it dawns on you that you've done:
> just the thought of undressing outdoors,
> exposing bare skin, makes you wince.

Mountaineers do not prepare for death, even if its possibility has crossed their minds. To prepare for it, to truly comprehend it, would render them helpless. Alison believed people usually only got hurt only when they lacked sufficient skills or good judgement. It was something she had to believe, perhaps, to go on climbing as a parent, as a mother.

I think of Laskey again, his poem steady with the rhythm of front crawl, a smooth arc through cold water:

And that's best, to have gone on swimming
easily to the end: your crawl
full of itself, and the future
no further than your folded towel.

A folded towel. A tent. A rucksack. The flags of base camp, flapping in the breeze.

K2 is an insistent triangle, a steep pyramid rising from a glacier, the highest point in the Karakoram range and the second highest mountain in the world. The rock is rusty brown, reddish, glimpsed through enveloping snow. The south face is more than 5 miles high. On a difficult mountain, it presents the most demanding route. There are 29 deaths per 100 safe returns, the second highest death rate after other 8,000-metre-plus peaks like Annapurna. K2 also became popularly known as 'the Savage Mountain' after George Bell – a climber on the 1953 American expedition – told reporters, 'It's a savage mountain that tries to kill you.' The foot of the mountain bears a shrine topped by a white cross and a series of plaques and memorials. The weather is notoriously fickle. Storms move in quickly and ravage the slopes. Even the approach to the mountain is particularly difficult, a long trudge up the bleak Baltoro Glacier. That's the landscape Alison entered less than three months after her triumphant return from Everest.

The sections from Alison's diaries quoted in *Regions of the Heart* as records of her last trip are full of anguish and ambivalence. By that point, she had been away from the children for months. At home, she pined for the mountains in a similar way, treating them like abandoned friends or lovers. What she experienced was a profound duality: always divided, always feeling she was in the wrong place. This is the purgatory of motherhood – perhaps of the human condition altogether – to want or need something else and then, as soon as you have it, to need the opposite. She wrote: 'It eats away at me – wanting the children and wanting K2 – I feel like I'm being pulled in two.'

Her time on K2 was frustrating, punctuated by storms that left climbers confined to their tents, fearing avalanches. Alison longed for the ascent to be over so that she could return home, but instead missed a chance to make a summit bid and had to stand by while news of other climbers' successes filtered down to her camp.

Finally, on 9 August 1995, the weather cleared. There was a window of opportunity, sharp and enticing.

The last entry in Alison's diary describes the pink sunset over Chogolisa, Broad Peak and K2, the banks of cloud behind, her hopes that the weather will hold just long enough for a last summit bid before she has to leave Pakistan. I imagine how she closed the pages and faced the morning, leaning into the dawn. All she needed was clear sky, a fair wind. One last push up the mountain and then home to Tom and Kate, the bread-scent and stickiness of their hugs, their soft, plump faces and wild stories. An afternoon walk down the glen with Tom running ahead of her, swiping at grasses and bracken with a stick, Kate ambling by her side. It was not much to ask. She had worked so tirelessly, endured so much hardship. She was sick of the mountain and – in that moment – sick of the company of climbers, the indifferent companionship of rock and ice. All she needed was a break. In the last throes of labour, I remember asking for a rest when rest was impossible. Just a second, just a moment's pause. But neither children nor mountains will let you rest.

The sky did not remain clear. When Alison stood on the summit of K2, rainclouds were already massing and rising from the valleys. Wind hit the foot of the mountain and was tunnelled up the face at hurricane-force speed. It became a howling storm, climbers flattening themselves against the ground and praying to be held. Alison was still high up, descending towards safety. A speck on the side of the mountain. The winds that peeled her from K2 were in excess of 140 miles per hour. Her body was never retrieved.

In 1992, three years before the expedition that would kill her, Alison Hargreaves had begun to suffer from strange attacks: she would be overwhelmed by exhaustion, heavy and listless. Then she would struggle to breathe, her skin becoming red and blotchy. When it passed, she was utterly spent, slumped like a climber at base camp, stumbling towards bed. In the aftermath of my own panic attacks, I thought of a day on Creag Meagaidh with my dad, a sudden white-out that engulfed and disoriented us, how we took a bearing but still almost ended up by the sheer rocks on one of the mountain sides. How easy it would have been to walk out into open air. Easy as letting a child fall from your arms at the top of a car park, letting your arms open and the air accept your precious cargo. I thought of blizzards and whipping snow, of snow caves collapsing, or what it would be like to be buried underground. And I thought of Alison's slender frame, the landscape accepting her slowly, layers of snow and sky.

/\/\/\/\/\/\/\ BELAY

It would not be fair to say that her body is an embarrassment to you. It is too abstract for that. A moving form, slow and methodical. She keeps a direct course, stopping every now and then as if rattled by something. To you, she is something like the clumped ferns on the ledge beside you, tips made rusty by the year, fixed in place but swaying slightly when the wind disturbs them, giving the air of stillness and motion all at once. She is not in a hurry. She wants to enjoy this.

Down in the pub, the fire will have been lit and boots placed on the hearth, treacle-coloured pints poured and left to settle. The barman will still be sweating from his morning cycle ride, 50 miles and back in time to pull his uniform on. A dog smell in the corners, the flagstones cool. The aftermath of last night's music. Once, a bird got trapped in the bar room and battered itself against the rafters, unable to see a way out, water unsettled from its wings, scattering in bright diamonds. It took one of the unspeaking farmers to rescue it, grab it and set it free. Soup smells. Wood burning. Old smoke. Weather clinging to everything, even indoors.

You are here but you are also down there. You do not know where you belong. When you get into the warmth, part of you will still be up here, shivering, waiting for her to catch up.

CARRYING A HEART

I have been carrying Alfie up mountains since he was a foetus. I liked to think of him, tiny, seahorse-strange, swimming in the darkness of my body while I strode through clear air. In the first trimester when motion and scent and colour still made me nauseous, I visited Scotland for a writing retreat. I was much too sick to write. The blinking pale screen made me think of porcelain, the sink I bent over each morning, vomiting away my breakfast. It was a calm, bright week in May, so I took off into the hills beyond Arrochar, wearing pyjama bottoms – the loosest trousers I had – and a borrowed waterproof, scandalously unprepared for mountains. Something about the scale of the Munros and Corbetts, their plateaus and peaks, calmed my nausea. I climbed Ben Vorlich and the Cobbler, scrambling up towards the rocky summit, using my hands. I took pride in overtaking groups of men who leaned heavily on their trekking poles, fighting for breath. I held the secret knowledge of my pregnancy, curled in my fingertips. I spoke to Alfie as I walked, harboured tentative dreams of taking him back to the Highlands as a child, pointing out these shapes on the horizon, showing him where he'd been before he was born. But I was furtive too, guilty in my knowledge. When I set up my camera and clambered onto a summit trig point for a photo, balancing on one leg, grinning and throwing my arms wide, I thought of my teenage stepdaughter, her concern about me climbing. 'Look after the baby,' everyone said. I knew that I was doing that. But for mothers, care is part performative, a public demonstration of caution. Your private risk assessment is never enough.

When I took Alfie to the Fells as a small baby, I wore him proudly on my chest as if his presence explained me. A friend with a toddler once described her devastation at walking into her favourite cafe with her tiny daughter, seeing old friends and realising she was now invisible to them, everyone cooing and smiling at the child. For me, it was different. When I strapped Alfie to my chest, he came before me, helped me forge a path through the day. He was my small, fierce trailblazer. I wanted people to look at him. Though I often have bright, dyed hair, though my arms are intricate with tattoos, though I sometimes announce myself with my clothes, I'm uncomfortable in the spotlight of someone's attention. The ink on my skin is at least part distraction: look at my designs, don't look deeper. It is the same when I write. Being candid on the page might (fairly) be judged as a display of something, a desire to be seen. But I want the impossible of my audience. I want them to read the book without scrutinising the author. I want to throw my voice, separate it from my body. What am I afraid of? That I will prove disappointing. That I might be even less interesting than I seem. The physical process of carrying a child seemed refreshingly uncomplicated in that sense. Holding my son gave me a straightforward purpose, one that everyone could understand, instantly. A world away from the usual complications of writing, publishing or simply walking around in a female body which might either be deemed too compelling or not compelling enough, too fat, too thin, too flat in places and too ample in others. My baby was straightforwardly loveable, his chubby legs appealing, his blue eyes sparking the right kind of mischief. Alfie made me walk taller, proud of his wan, ready smile and his expressive eyebrows, his new, fascinating face.

I loved the ceremony of wiggling him into the baby carrier and wrapping us both in a large coat, nodding to walkers as I passed them. His warmth and weight soon made me sweaty. We were welded together by our body heat. Our first excursions as a pair were on Stanage, a slow trudge up from the car park, snaking our way along its gritstone back. Stanage is scoured by wind and I was often nervous in the face of it, longed to shelter Alfie from the elements. I would dare myself to walk further each time before I turned back. We walked with sheep and curlews, the bubbling call of a grouse. He was my lamb, meek and sleeping on my chest. When he was two months old, I carried him up Win Hill in the Peak District, taking the steepest way from Bamford, a short, sharp slog. I picked my way over tree roots, placing my feet with care. I had never been so deliberate. The route follows a trickle of a path through dense woodland, then opens out to a broad track, mottled with stones. From the summit, we could see the Great Ridge over to Mam Tor, the reservoirs at Ladybower, paths yearning in every direction. My photographs from that day are strangely flat, giving no sense of height and exposure. But the gusts and the sun's knife made everything feel precarious, temporary. I took Alfie out of the sling and fed him, snuggled in my down jacket.

Alfie was four months old when we climbed Cat Bells and Blencathra in the Lake District. Blencathra is a slumbering dog of a hill, a huge beast with teeth – many walkers have got into difficulty on Sharp Edge, a rising crest of naked rock that tops the mountain. I chose an easy route from the village of Threlkeld, gaining a gentler ridge through ferns. Jess came with me but I took the lead. It was a leaden morning, sun cutting through only briefly. Blencathra was steeper than I remembered. My back ached with every step, weighed down by Alfie in his blue suit, an outfit my dad had described as *bazzin'*, meaning *smart, impressive, showy*. We were pummelled by wind and Alfie began to howl, but at other times he was alert and curious, swivelling his head to take in the open land below. He was facing outwards, towards the mountain. I tried not to think about the consequences of a slip, his cheeks against scree. Only days afterwards, Jess told me he had found it terrifying, had wondered at my sanity. Later in the summer, I took the steam train to Rhyd Ddu from Porthmadog with my friend Alan and set off to climb Snowdon. Alfie was on my back this time, his legs hugging me. He was old enough by then to be delighted by the scenery, curious and bird-like. We stopped for snacks and Alfie crawled in the grass, grinning, covering his yellow top and striped leggings with dirt and prickly leaves. The route we had chosen was the least popular on the mountain, a gentle zig-zagging path followed by a stretch of dramatic ridge walking. I felt Alfie's weight with every step. A raven wheeled overhead, pointing the compass of its body to the top. Alan took a picture of me near the summit, flanked by minarets and spires of rock: a woman with pink hair and red cheeks, looking bashfully at the camera, and a plump, contented baby, his mouth wide with glee. But strangers eyed us with wary interest.

Have you walked all the way?
He's got the right idea!
Can you carry me too?
Is he warm enough like that?

Most assumed that Alan was the father, jokily berated him for letting his girlfriend do the hard work. I didn't bother to correct them: I felt embarrassed, even though the misunderstanding was theirs. We must have made a striking spectacle, tall, lean Alan with his long black hair and sculpted beard, me with my patterned skin and piercings, my chubby, giggling cargo. I wanted to grip the arms of those strangers, look them in the eye, hiss something in answer. This should not be a surprise. It's often women who carry the most.

What do we take with us into the mountains? There is a stark hierarchy of load-carrying. It is seldom comfortable to think about. In 2014, the deaths of 16 high-altitude workers, mostly Sherpas, on Everest brought arguments about the economy of weight, the commercial side of high-altitude mountaineering, into sharp focus. The Sherpas lost their lives while working, some as 'icefall doctors' (setting the ropes and ladders for expeditions to come through) in the Khumbu Icefall, the most dangerous part of the mountain. It was the biggest loss of life in a single event recorded on Everest up to that point. In the aftermath, some Sherpas went on strike, refusing to return to the mountain, disrupting planned expeditions. Some at base camp branded them selfish, others supported their stance. Most of the climbing community had turned their backs on Everest long ago.

Many Sherpas from the villages high in the mountains or the foothills of Nepal have turned to the industry as a means of survival, the region relying on Everest tourism. Every year close to 60,000 people visit this region to walk and stare at the world's tallest mountain. But the logistical and physical support, the load-carrying, comes from locals. Porters – thousands of them – are at the heart of the trekking industry, and it is on their backs that most of the equipment in the hills is carried, from television sets to beer and souvenirs. Sometimes, there is pressure to work without sufficient breaks, go too high too fast, risking altitude sickness. After the tragedy, a Kathmandu-based journalist called Jemima Diki Sherpa wrote an article about her experience of being 'a post arts-degree twentysomething' city girl with a Sherpa heritage, the expectations attached to her name. When she went to university in New Zealand, the first reaction elicited by her surname was 'How much can you carry?' She describes a childhood defined by lack of interest in mountains, getting Nuptse and Lhotse mixed up, and yet tragedy encroached on her everyday life, the deaths of relatives and acquaintances:

> As a young high-altitude expedition worker, the more you carry, the more you are paid. There is a per kilo equation for payment, and there is value, both in hard cash and in securing future work, in proving you are good. Do so, and you get hired the next season, possibly by one of the better companies, climbing literally up the mountain and figuratively up the ranks.

The best way to do all this is to move fast, carry the heaviest loads: double, triple. And the best way to do that is to dance, possibly unclipped, across the icefall ladders, putting yourself in grave danger. Mountaineering is an activity that demands a heavy load. Someone has to shoulder it: ropes and technical equipment, food and water, communications gear. It is stark, simple. Then there are the thoughts we take with us, the responsibilities, the sense of what we need to shoulder: financial pressures, family duty. When Alison Hargreaves climbed

Everest unsupported, she didn't have the help of Sherpas, carrying her own equipment up the mountain. But as a mother, in the eyes of those scrutinising her, she also carried a responsibility that her male counterparts did not. Some theorists talk about the 'mental load' of mothering, the inability to switch off, the way motherhood is always with you. The logistics of expeditions away from home are difficult for any mountaineer, financially and practically. But there is a further emotional burden taken into the hills by mothers, the weight of guilt. It simmers under the surface, breaks out in headlines like the ones that followed Alison's death: 'K2 Is Not for Mothers'. 'Was Brave Alison Such a Responsible Mother?' Mountaineering fathers are seldom subjected to this kind of scrutiny (except by themselves). Nor are their memoirs filled with the same anguished admissions and justifications, the same struggles to find space to train or chances to go away. In the eyes of the world, they are allowed to be athletes and parents simultaneously, or even athletes first and parents after.

When Alison became a climber as a teenage girl, she was joining an overwhelmingly male tradition. Women have been climbing pioneering routes since the 1800s, but always in small numbers. The first mountaineers like Lucy Walker in the Alps wore heavy crinoline skirts, lived on a diet of champagne and sponge cake in the hills. It is almost comical, absurd. Notoriously, one female climber took her skirt off to ascend the mountain in trousers, intending to put it on again when she returned. She had almost reached the town when she realised with horror her ladylike outfit remained behind a rock higher up the valley and had to go back for it. Women carried the baggage of feminine clothing.

In 2012, I hiked around Switzerland wearing a replica crinoline dress in homage to Victorian hiker Jemima Morrell, a young woman from Yorkshire who joined the first Thomas Cook tour of the Alps. My skirts were royal blue, my sleeves puffed – it was a more ornate outfit than the one Jemima would have worn, but it changed the space I occupied. Sitting on chairs was impossible, squeezing through doorways a challenge. Worse, even in the post-millennium era I was expected to take part in publicity photos for the trip in my bikini when we had breakfast at the hot springs in Leukerbad. I could not smile as the cameras flashed. I got out of the pool, threw on a pair of combat trousers and a jumper and set off alone into the Gemmi Pass, meeting the rest of the group (who travelled by cable car) at the top. With every step, I thought of lace and heavy cotton, imagined myself drowning in the fabrics women like Jemima had to wear, dresses the shape of upside-down flowers. I walked faster, breathing hard, up to the snow line. In 1859, Mrs Henry Warwick Cole had remarked dryly: 'A lady's dress is inconvenient for mountaineering.'

It's easy for these accounts of pioneering female climbers and other athletes to become anecdote and whimsy, earn laughter at dinner parties. I can reel off a litany of ludicrous stories: in his book *Mountaineering Women*, David Mazel describes 'Bob', 'the imaginary character invented by women climbers tired of hearing unsolicited advice from male passersby . . .' Even when women succeeded in their endeavours, they were often mocked or eyed suspiciously. 'The Grépon has disappeared,' said Etienne Bruhl in 1929. 'Of course, there are still some rocks standing there, but as a climb it no longer exists. Now that it has been done by two women alone, no self-respecting man can undertake it.' When Frenchwoman Anne Bernard applied to join the 1922 Everest expedition, the selection panel replied: 'It is impossible for the Mount Everest Committee to contemplate the application of a lady of whatever nationality to take part in a future expedition to Everest. The difficulties would be too great.'

We're more likely to have heard these stories – witty in their telling, recited comfortably – than to know about the life of Polish climber Wanda Rutkiewicz, who organised women-only expeditions to Himalayan peaks like Nanga Parbat, and became the first woman to climb K2, or Japanese housewife Junko Tabei, who climbed Everest in 1975. In the late 1970s when Alison entered the world of Peak District climbing, it is no surprise that she found it overwhelmingly macho. Men in patched-up down jackets, hanging out at the crags, leading difficult routes that they'd pore over later with pints in the pub. One traditional image of a British climber was someone like Don Whillans, a tough, recalcitrant working-class man from Salford, a heavy drinker and brawler. The scene was anarchic, hard-edged, competitive: climbers eking out their dole money in greasy-spoon cafes when it was too rainy to go to the crags, smoking roll-ups, sporting well-worn sweaters. The air teemed with smoke and tall stories, accounts of dangerous climbs and drunken dares. Some women climbed with their boyfriends, but few had independent ambitions that they would express in the bars and cafes around Hathersage and Stoney Middleton. A young woman like Alison was something of a curiosity. And when women are in a minority in a sport like climbing, they may be forced into competition with one another.

Alison had always gravitated towards climbing with women: her first partner was her schoolfriend Bev England. But she hadn't particularly interrogated the masculine culture she was part of: Bev and Alison did not even really think of themselves as unusual until other climbers commented on the rarity of seeing a 'pair of lasses' at the crag. They were just doing routes. They felt their motives for climbing weren't any different from those of their male contemporaries. In the early 1980s, when Alison was beginning to attract attention for her bold ascents in the UK, her ambition and tenacity, the British Mountaineering Council invited her to be part of one of the first International Women's Climbing Meets to be held in the UK, a select group of 20 women. It was a whirlwind climbing tour of Britain, a meet but also a press trip designed to shine a spotlight on women's climbing. Many of the women on the meet were politically engaged, approaching their sport from a feminist perspective. Jill Lawrence, one of the leading figures on the trip, was an academic lesbian feminist who raised her eyebrows when Alison's older boyfriend turned up at the crags or hung around taking photos. Alison's youth and apparent naivety were challenged: was she only free to climb because she had moved in with a business owner 16 years her senior? Reading about the press trip in *Regions of the Heart*, I realised how much I take for granted in an age where the all-female Pinnacle Club is celebrating its centenary, where climbing is a mainstream leisure activity for many.

Towards the end of the meet, Douglas and Rose report that some of the women visited Higgar Tor, a small outcrop, dwarfed by the bigger edges of Stanage and Burbage nearby, but home to notoriously difficult routes. Jill Lawrence and her girlfriend, Rosie Jakes, had their sights set on the Rasp, a brutal overhang that tests the climber's ability to hold on, legs swinging in space. It has always terrified me, unsettled me. All my memories of Higgar are of midge clouds and bleeding hands. Rosie and Jill both tried the route and placed protection on it but fell off. Alison – limbs fresh – was able to clip into the gear and concentrate on the gymnastics and dance of climbing. She reached the top, proving herself on a gritstone 'test piece'. While the word around the scene was that she had excelled on a tough route, others were disgruntled, feeling that Alison had 'stolen' the route from Jill and unfairly claimed glory. As Ed Douglas and David Rose put it:

> Whatever the truth, some of Lawrence's friends believed Alison had gone too far by attempting to overshadow her elders and betters. She was forcefully criticized, mainly in her absence. As time went on, the story grew in the telling, becoming the start of a largely undeserved reputation for hyperbole amongst some climbers which Alison would find extremely difficult to lose.

As they go on to note, the fellowship of women had a mixed effect on Alison in this particular case. During the meet, she'd been able to discover her climbing potential, leading routes that she might otherwise have been afraid of. But there was also a mounting sense of pressure and expectation, of public scrutiny. And, through the meet, she discovered how female competition and jealousy could overwhelm camaraderie, how divisive gendered climbing experiences could be. In her own career as a mountaineer, she had frequent moments of self-doubt and jealousy, like her envy of Catherine Destivelle when Catherine soloed the Eiger. She was similarly annoyed when Rebecca Stephens became the first British woman to reach the summit of Everest. Throughout her life, women – like her long-term friend and climbing partner, Bev – were a source of companionship and support, but they were also her rivals. Perhaps that was inevitable in a structure that affords fewer opportunities to women, forces them to compete. As a mother to young children, Alison had few female friends to help her and as a climber she was sometimes isolated, comparing herself to others. Her climbing relationships with men must often have seemed simpler.

The desire to enter a fellowship of men is something I understand, something I felt acutely before I became a mother. In my early 20s, I found myself adrift in Derbyshire, finishing my PhD, desperate for the company of gorse and stone and heather. As a teenager, my dad had always let me join in with his Highland walking trips with friends. I was a girl among middle-aged men, priding myself on my enthusiasm, my ability to keep up with them (even outpace them) in the hills, my taste for real ale and whisky in the evenings. I enjoyed the simplicity of their company, their capacity for pleasing themselves, the way conversation so often circled around route planning, climbing anecdotes, the immediate landscape. I loved the way they inhabited each moment, savoured drives at dusk with the Glen Shiel Horseshoe in the background, a cold pint of Schiehallion after a long walk. They catalogued their lives by mountains, by ascents. I found myself comparing their raucous laughter and dogged endurance in the hills to the complicating presence of my mum back at home. I wanted to be a man in the mountains, capable and calm. So when I found myself looking for rock-climbing partners as a PhD student, I gravitated towards men my dad's age, to banter and brutal focus.

I joined the Derbyshire Irregulars Climbing Society – DICS for short. On a muggy summer evening just after I'd been introduced to them, I found myself roped up on a gentle slab at Baslow Edge, the rocks choked by foliage and overgrown trees. I was traversing left and needed to take a big step, a move that threatened to unbalance me. I seemed to pause there for an eternity, listening to the clank of gear and the chimes of laughter further down the crag, the easy sounds of men climbing together. I swayed back and forth slightly, apologising to my belay partner, mustering courage to commit to the move. I was sweating and flustered, hardly any distance off the ground, frustrated by my own ambivalence. I heard two of the group stalwarts walking down the descent route after finishing their climb, moving slowly under the weight of their ropes and gear. Then, as they passed me, I heard a low whistle and a jokey cry of, 'Great view you're giving us, Hels!' I laughed, blushed beneath my orange helmet, felt my palms dampen, quivered like a deer who wants to take flight. Climbing with men made me acutely aware of my hips and bottom, my shape in jeans and hiking trousers. Part of me wanted to diminish it, hide it under cascading skirts. Part of me felt I should be able to wear tight leggings under my climbing harness, that my body on rock should be unremarkable.

On a trip to Kalymnos in 2013, I joined an all-male climbing party, men my dad's age and a bit younger. The Greek limestone cliffs were more enticing than any rock

I'd ever seen before: some shaped like castles, some arching towards the sunset, huge caves and tufa shaped like icicles. The sun scorched everything in its path, whittled the landscape down to scant shadows. The sea – once popular for sponge diving – was cartoon blue. The village's shops were stuffed with thyme and honey, the bars draped with moonlight. It was one of the best weeks of my life. I was in my element. We climbed sport routes all day – clipping into artificial bolts – and gorged on Mythos beer and Greek salad in the evenings, watching the shimmering path made by the ferry to Telendos, a conical island out in the Aegean Sea. I climbed out of my skin each morning, watched by the oldest in our group.

'We'll have to call you Troy on this trip,' he said. 'Make you an honorary boy.'

On the last day, another friend joked about the benefits of belaying me, how he preferred my arse to the lads'. I had been flattered to be branded Troy. It didn't make me feel like one of the boys, it made me feel genderless, as if my gender could be ignored. Perhaps that's the experience of being a male climber, your sex unremarkable, your body functional, fluid on the rock. But I had been conditioned to treat a comment about my physique as a compliment. No matter how much my ears burned, I had to smile. And – regardless of the sexual politics – I loved climbing with men, loved the narrowness of their focus. I loved the way we mostly kept our talk to the routes and the beta, how I knew what they looked like when they were most afraid but barely knew what jobs they did or who their families were. Our climbing relationships were workmanlike, framed by a pragmatic intimacy. And I was humbled by their kindness and encouragement, how the DICS lent me climbing gear and built my confidence, belayed me patiently through freezing days on Stanage, gifted me books, taught me rope skills, told me what I was capable of. I owe so much to my climbing mentors and friends and so little of it felt interrupted by gender. They accepted me with compassion, good humour and wisdom. They are friends for life, companions who care unconditionally about one another.

It's my own motives for joining an overwhelmingly male climbing group that I've questioned. Ever since I was a buck-toothed, straw-haired child, I've been afraid of other girls. I always sensed myself as a fraud, a bad example of femininity. My best friend at primary school mocked my clothes, the tie-dyed trousers and the wildlife

T-shirts my mum used to dress me in. I didn't know about TV and pop music, didn't have posters of footballers on my walls. I had to learn to integrate myself, learning lyrics by the Spice Girls, cutting out images of Michael Owen and attaching them to my wardrobe with Blu Tack. When we played pretend pop stars, the other girls always made me be Sporty Spice, the one considered a tomboy. I was serious and bookish, spent hours in the playground rescuing worms, scooping them from puddles and mud, afraid that they would be trodden on. At secondary school, I was the laughing-stock of my friendship group, felt chills spread from my stomach each time I entered the classroom and found the girls whispering about me, mock-giggling under their hands. I was a swot, a boy, a 'lesbo'. I was ugly, first too fat and then too thin. I began spending lunchtimes in the library or running laps of the field, leaving my snacks uneaten in my bag. I spent time with the boy who everyone teased for being gay and the girl whose clothes smelled. Groups of girls – even groups of women – have always brought back the smell of sherbet and Body Shop strawberry lip balm, goodies that weren't often shared with me.

*

During my pregnancy, Jess and I signed up for a National Childbirth Trust course in Sheffield as a way of meeting other expecting couples. The meetings took place in a dusty classroom set back from the bustle of Abbeydale Road. Shifting uncomfortably on my chair, I eyed the other women with suspicion, looked for signs of glamour, attractiveness, unfriendliness. My cropped pink hair made me self-conscious and I wished I'd smothered it with a hat. Within the first hour, the women and men had been segregated, split into groups to discuss their feelings about pregnancy and our impending due dates. My eyes kept darting towards Jess across the room. There was laughter. The men seemed relaxed, the women earnest. To close the meeting, the group leader passed a loaded rucksack round which represented the weight of a baby. Each man was asked to wear it in turn, experience what we carried. They murmured humbly, made sheepish jokes. Then they took it off again. They sat down, released.

The flurry of activity on our WhatsApp group terrified me at first. I typed comments and deleted them, convinced I was in danger of saying something wrong. At our first social event – cake and non-alcoholic prosecco at someone's house – I gripped the stem of my glass tightly.

My bump was too small, my conversation stilted. We were all around 30, living in a leafy suburb. We had friends and cafes and TV shows and privilege in common. But I did not feel like a mother. I barely felt like a woman. As the others joked and talked, I tried to arrange my face in the right expressions – sympathy, amusement. I curated my body language. I imagined everyone could see through me, how I was acting out womanhood with my gel-manicured nails – inappropriate for climbing – and my pre-planned questions. I wanted to run out into the darkness, up the unlit hill to Ringinglow Road, through the night to Lady Cannings Plantation, the shrouded comfort of the trees, their lovely conspiracy. Now, my inner dialogue seems like arrogance. As if I was the only person to feel that way.

There is an intimacy that comes from seeing another woman's photograph just after they've given birth, red-faced, hair plastered with sweat, newborn curled and livid on their breast. As the first babies arrived, I marvelled at the pictures, the wide eyes and fixed smiles of new motherhood, the almost eerie aura of calm. Each birth photo made me cry. In the days after Alfie's arrival, I shared my joy, fear and bottomless sorrow with the women I'd half feared on our first meeting. I said their names like a litany: Susan, Sarah, Charlotte, Rosie, Chloe, Milly, Simona. It became my midnight incantation, a reminder that I was not alone. I discovered the indescribable tenderness and closeness that comes from sharing sticky Calpol dawns and 3am TV, insatiable cake cravings, sore breasts and weeping stitches, colic and winter colds and cluster feeding. We texted through the night, met in parks with our babies swaddled in knitted blankets and fleeces, helped each other with GP appointments and impossible nap times and broken afternoons. We could over-share and nobody minded. We met in kitchens and church halls and retail parks and coffee shops, our cheeks sallow and our eyes underscored by shadow. We took walks in winter weather, bracing our bodies against the wind. Together, we formed a shield. As the babies became stronger, bigger, angrier, funnier, we began to know each other as women as well as mothers, exchanging stories about the lives we had before pregnancy. When Alfie was four months old, I launched my first novel at a bookshop in the city centre. One by one, the NCT couples filed through the door, pushing prams or wearing slings. The launch was punctuated by burbles and screams. I was delighted, close to tears.

Those months of sleep deprivation and keening worry made me raw, skinless almost. Some days I seemed to float through the world, my actions automatic, my lips barely moving. Other days I was jittery and wild, walking for miles with the pram, clutching Alfie too tightly. My new friends never laughed at me, never ignored my garbled calls for help. We talked about everything: postpartum sex and mastitis, the anxiety of routine hospital appointments. We raged and cried to each other when it felt as if sleep was a room we were locked out of for ever. One woman's son would not sleep without her next to him. Another's baby was allergic to his formula milk. One woman's daughter was rushed back to hospital with suspected meningitis. Each agony was felt collectively, each small triumph celebrated. We pored over the distance that seemed to yawn between us and our partners in those early months. I texted them lines from Liz Berry's 'Sky Birth':

> Bringing you to the world, I let the mountain enter me:
>
> mauve, shadow, the sky a zoetrope spinning crows
>
> and rain-soaked fog.

We all felt like that some days – porous, rain-clogged, heavy. The landscape had entered us, we carried our surroundings with us, became sensitive to light and humidity, frost and sunrise. Our nights lasted for ever. We shared books, podcasts with comforting, velvet-voiced narrators, TV shows about baby animals. One was a programme about a man who fed orphaned Russian bear cubs in a cabin in the northern forests. When he tried to sleep, the cubs woke him with squeals and scuffling and he rose at hourly intervals to feed them from a bottle. I loved the eager tilt of their heads, the bright punctuation of their eyes, their sturdy bodies and their curved claws. When they were strong enough, their keeper opened the cabin door and let the white light of the snow fill it. One by one, the bears shambled to the doorway and sniffed the air, testing it. Then they touched the ground with outstretched paws, retracted them again. I was one of their number then, trembling on the threshold, sensing freedom in bark and berries, moss and musk. I felt my whole body quiver. The other women were my litter mates, my pack, my comfort. On the screen, I watched one bear take the lead, padding carefully towards the pines. The others followed then, compact, dark, bunched with life.

Motherhood made me trust other women in a way I had never been able to before. Through Alfie, I felt bonded to them. We all had different interests, distinct passions: allotments and gym classes, nights out and book clubs. Milly had once been a champion sailor, steering boats halfway around the world. Simona came from Lithuania via London and Berlin, had married in Las Vegas. Rosie described her year backpacking round New Zealand and I felt encouraged to talk about my expedition to Greenland, my love of mountains and edges. Nobody else climbed, but they were fascinated. As a young woman, I'd learned that difference made you vulnerable. At university, I joined mountaineering clubs and went to real ale pubs where I could talk to men about climbing. I was preoccupied with groups of women, an outsider, imagining them whispering behind my back. Even as an adult, I was stuck in the playground, fearful and blushing, the wrong shape and size and voice and accent, holding the wrong words in my mouth, making the wrong gestures, loving the wrong things. It took Alfie's birth to give me a sustained, meaningful experience of female kinship, a group where differences were points of interest, where I could talk freely about climbs, the adventures I'd dragged my body on over the years. I felt true friendship. And as I began to long for gritstone again, for pain in my fingertips and acid in my muscles, I dreamed of climbing with another woman, something I'd barely done before. It took me until he was a year old to manage it.

I met Anna Fleming in the Dennis Knoll car park on a spring day so wet the rock was weeping, green sodden corners, secret pockets of water. Anna is a writer like me and we'd shared stories of climbs for months, plotted ways to meet up. It was an inauspicious Sunday, cool and breezy, the horizon soggy. Stanage was a faint line drawn by a shaky hand. But the whole day is luminous in recollection. I remember curlews, chicks in the grass near the verge, confident and downy. A dust everywhere in the air that might have been fine rain or midges. A Christian meditation group making their way up to the crag from the car park, stately and poised in white robes. Their bright insistence against the gloom, sombre procession. On the edge, grouped together, they became earthed clouds.

I remember my return to leading, my first attempts since pregnancy: the sharp line of Tango Crack at High Neb, jamming my foot awkwardly, forcing my hands into dank rock. I remember reacquainting myself with cams, their satisfying bite. The direct line to the sky I made with my body, each move a minor prayer. I remember how easily we took turns, sharing the leads. Anna swearing, her infectious laugh. Her lithe, tall shape and her elegant, thoughtful movements. How, as I watched her, I could imagine my body making those same shapes. In Tango Crack, we couldn't dislodge my purple cam and had to leave it behind. It felt like an offering to the rock, to the wide, grey day. I almost liked to think of it there, jammed for ever, or until some other climber wriggled it out and took it home as a trophy.

We were the only women climbing together that day. Our last route of the afternoon was an off-width chimney, devious and humbling. It forced our bodies into awkward angles, splayed then cramped. It trapped us, hemmed us in and then spat us out again. We revelled in it, bonded by misadventure. All the while, a bearded man beside us was teaching his young daughter how to climb, his shouted instructions – 'Keep that tension in your body!' – and her nervous reply, her feet slipping underneath her, the morning giving way. She was slender and quick, determined. Another group of men – mid-20s with gym-built bodies –

were packing their gear away, appraising their trip. 'It was OK,' said one. 'The climbs were mostly vanilla.' I turned away from them, back towards the slickness of the rock, back towards the rope that linked me to Anna. We had never belayed each other before today, but I was climbing more confidently than I ever had, enjoying the scant holds and polished rock. I trusted Anna utterly, implicitly. I knew she would hold my fall.

/\/\/\/\/\/\/\/\

TOPPING OUT

Patchwork. Jigsaw. Tapestry. There are so many ways of describing the ground seen from above, but none of them are right. It is more disconnected than that, not stitched together but layered. Grass chucked on earth. Trees perched on grass. Leaves a scattered afterthought. Boulders thrown down. Rivers poured in. You focus on the movement of a farmer's jeep down a single track, a plume trailing from the exhaust. Toy houses. Farms that seem so small you could lift them on a finger. Here, rock is larger than life and everything left at ground level is insubstantial.

This is it. Whenever you reach the top of a route, you are reminded that climbing is a pointless activity. What can you see from here that you couldn't see on the ascent, from the first pitch, first ledge? The quality of the air is no different. You are breathing a little harder, but your body is unchanged. What do you know that you didn't know before? What has the sequence taught you? You spend your life moving in graceful circles, reaching safety only to leave it behind again, a long, looping pattern of ascent and descent. Chasing your own shadow.

You remember childhood scrambles in Wales and Scotland, the pitiful weather, the lactic acid in your thighs and the rain plastering your fringe to your face, how you'd dream of the summit all the way up, look forward to taking out your silver thermos and eating your squashed sandwiches up there, only to find it was too wind-scoured to sit down, too cold to linger, too misty to make out the hunched shapes of other mountains, old men around a dominoes table, weary and only half proud.

You are whistling again, trying to coax the valley to join in. A finale must have music. You move your right leg slightly and a pebble clatters into space. This will be your orchestra. Stone fall. Metal on metal. The sharp, staccato sounds of the day. The river in the distance, barely mumbling. A rumble that could be traffic or rock tumbling. Steady breath and the heart ferrying blood around the body.

If you can find meaning in climbing, you can find meaning in life. Hand, hand. Foot, foot. Pitch after pitch in the stifling afternoon. You love it precisely because it means nothing.

DREAMERS OF THE DAY

'The dreamers of the day are dangerous men, for they may act their dream with open eyes, to make it possible.'

– T.E. Lawrence

2020

It is spring, the UK gripped by the coronavirus pandemic, shops closed and roads eerily silent. Alfie took his first, tentative outdoor steps when the daffodils came, the verges sickly yellow, the air too warm for March. Now, he's gaining confidence. For months, he has been hauling himself up on furniture, cruising around the living room, yelping with frustration at each fall. Our first outdoor walks were gentle, but he was soon trying to run, charging up and down the garden path, careering through the flats behind our house, somersaulting down a hill in Chelsea Park and scuffing his chin. Strolls around the neighbourhood became walks in the woods. Walks in the woods became gleeful scrambles over tree routes, muddy hands and holes in trousers. He is a stone, gathering moss, unstoppable downhill.

As soon as it is allowed, I drive him to Burbage Edge, the verge of the Peak District, and set him down on the track. The path towards the brook is steep and littered with obstacles, uneven and precarious. He wrinkles his nose at me, points towards the shapes of Higgar Tor, monstrous from this angle, squat and menacing, looming between us and the sun. 'Rocks, Alfie,' I whisper. 'Beautiful.' He beams toothily. I kid myself that he understands. Then he is off, sturdy legs motoring, too fast for his body. Toddlers are so improbable, each movement hard won. When we reach the bridge, he whimpers to be lifted up onto a high boulder, wanting to see the charge of water close up. I hesitate, place him on top of the stone, hands ready to catch him if he slips. The brook is muscular, bullying its way downhill. He turns to me and at first the water muffles his single word. Then he repeats it: ''Appy.' He always drops the *h*. His way of communicating joy is just like the way he says his own name. I love their interchangeable nature, how easily he is moved to praise. 'Alfie. 'Appy.' When he says it, I hug my arms around my own body as if I'm trying to stop myself bursting with affection, with adoration for my small friend, my brave dependent boy whose independence suddenly seems real to me.

The path shelves towards the Fox House pub, smooth in places, dotted with shining puddles. Sometimes, I have to carry Alfie, but when we reach a dense clutch of boulders under Ash Tree Wall, a place I've often climbed, he quivers with excitement, asks to get down again. I place him on the ground and he toddles towards a small, gently angled slab, looking back to make sure I'm watching. The way up is too sheer, but he can clumsily traverse across it. He leans to his left, body tensed with effort, then retracts his hand again. He does not scrabble for holds but considers the move carefully, face set with concentration. I see the man in his child's face and I almost recoil. He can't quite commit to the move. He glances to me again for reassurance. I am already anticipating the crash, the indignity, him stranded like a beetle on its back. He tries to move his foot wide for purchase.

In climbing, we'd call that bridging. When he steadies himself and moves, inching across to the other side, my relief is palpable.

To me, just for a moment, he is the famous free soloist Alex Honnold on El Capitan, reaching the crux, executing a perfect karate kick move, the sudden precariousness of it, the reality of the fall. Love knows no canvas. It does not respect the aptness of metaphor. It is particular, urgent and dictatorial. It is melodramatic, intense and ridiculous. It makes me watch my son and see the swoop of El Capitan's Freerider route, makes me hold my breath the way I do when I watch films of Alex Honnold without ropes, his spider-like fluency. Alex is the same age as me, and yet whenever I see him on television or in photos, he's somehow boyish. I find myself questioning what his mother Dierdre Wolownick thinks of his daring solos. Dierdre is a climber too and has written movingly about the process of both climbing with her son and following his career. She knows what it is to fall. She says that Alex never tells her about his big climbs before they happen. Imagination, she says, is both a blessing and a curse. Without it, her son might not risk death on such a regular basis. But would he be really alive? Or would he be biding time, uninspired by life? She notes dryly that 'dying takes many forms'. Only the climber can evaluate the risk of the climb:

> That's where trust comes in. Eventually, parents have to trust their children's judgment, whether about money, job, child care, homes, or so many of the things life throws at us. Climbing is Alex's job. And I trust his judgment.

The umbilical cord as a rope that remains, invisible and strong, linking parent and child. First, Alfie was part of my body. Then he was cradled in my arms, attached to my breast, comforted by my voice and scent. Then he held my hand as we walked together. Now, he is stretching the elastic between us, ranging further, becoming independent. He is ready. I am only holding him back.

One day towards the end of my pregnancy, when the city seemed unrelenting, claggy with mist and dead leaves, I drove into Sheffield and passed the Climbing Works, the indoor centre where I used to boulder, testing my nerve and muscles on the overhanging walls, the sparse neon holds. For a moment in the car, I allowed myself to switch off the static of anxiety I live with daily, and imagine a happy future: me climbing with my boy, holding his ropes, watching him fluid and happy, confident in his element. I smiled as I idled at the traffic lights, took my hands off the wheel for a moment and placed them on the swell of my belly, felt Alfie buck and kick. By the time the lights had changed, my face had clouded. What if he was talented? What if he took risks? What if he climbed at altitude? What if he fell, was injured or even killed? I knew I would never be able to describe this mix of dread and joy to anyone, in the same way I'd always struggled to explain my love of rock climbing to my family, how I was drawn to it even though it made me quiver with nerves. I wondered how Alison Hargreaves would have felt watching her son Tom's bold progress as a climber if she'd lived long enough. Imagining it seems almost an act of violence. No mother wants to see their child fall.

I go back to my books, scouring her relationship with Tom as a child for clues. Did she worry about him as a toddler, the way I fear for Alfie? Did she let him roam regardless? Whatever anxieties may have lingered in the background, Tom Ballard was raised to love the hills, to see them as his territory, his playground. His first climb was in France when he was just five years old. He climbed up a limestone slab in the Calanques barefoot, encouraged by his father, scampering easily to the top. When Alison reached the pair and saw Tom she was perturbed, torn between wanting to let her child explore and fearing for his safety. She argued with Jim afterwards, back at the tent. I can visualise that moment beneath the slab perfectly, the look passing between husband and wife, her reproach and his shrug, Tom's excited chatter in the background, utterly oblivious to the adult world.

Tom's childhood had been dominated by mountains, long before he learned to scale them, his existence often itinerant. Travelling the globe and scrambling over rocks was simply Tom's idea of fun. When the Ballard family moved to Fort William in Scotland in the 1990s, Tom's new teacher at school tried to integrate him into the class by asking him where he'd been living before. 'Everest base camp,' replied Tom, deadpan. The classroom rippled. Tom was already staring out of the window, imagining what it would take to climb over the gates into open space, bracken and burns and snowscapes. He tolerated school, preferring to be outside, climbing or skiing. Pictures from that era often show him and Kate in ski lifts beside their mother, probably in the Cairngorms, Tom grinning from ear to ear. He was seldom still. When he was still young, someone once likened his fluid movement on a mountain to George Best's dexterity on a football pitch. And from an early age, he was soloing rock routes around their family home in Scotland. Home was not a town, an address or a cottage. It was a kind of landscape, the urgency of rock, the impassivity of ice.

As a young man of 26, in an interview with Robert Chalmers, Tom Ballard was very clear that he felt children should not on principle be protected from danger. When the journalist mentioned that he was nervous about his own son taking up climbing (a friend of Robert's had died on an easy route in the Peak District in a freak accident), Tom replied that accidents often happen when you least expect, on easy descent routes, times when you've lost concentration. His comments echoed Alison's certainty that climbing was as safe as driving a car. He added:

> Up on the mountain, I feel totally at ease. It's down here that I feel uncomfortable. I am regularly asked, 'What do you think about when you're climbing a mountain: your mother?' To which I say, 'No. Oddly enough I am thinking mainly about not falling off.'

It wasn't just Belper and Fort William that got him accustomed to climbing. He was also introduced to the world of international climbing from an early age, to the nomadic existence of the high-altitude mountaineer. There is a peculiar comfort in its privations, simplicity in the daily business of survival, getting enough water for tea, enough warmth, enough food. Tom and Kate must have been curiosities at base camp on expeditions with their mother, plucky and bold, hunkering down in their sleeping bags or playing by day in the snow, building ramps and castles. I imagine them roaming, the Alps and foothills becoming their vast playground, washing in rivers and eating under the light of the stars.

All that ended abruptly when their mother never returned from Pakistan. I think of their remote Scottish house, the telephone ringing and Jim Ballard answering it, hand gripping the receiver too tightly, the sound of the children playing in the background, feet clattering down the hall, running towards their father eager for news of Alison.

'It was the hardest thing I've ever had to do,' Jim said later of that afternoon. 'I explained very simply that mummy was lost in the mountains and had died. Kate, who was only four, dissolved into tears straightaway.'

Tom, he claimed, tried to be 'much tougher' about it. And in the painful aftermath, it was Tom who asked his father if they could go and see her final resting place, set the long voyage to Pakistan by rail and plane and by foot in motion. He took his beloved Brown Bear with him on the journey, a plump teddy with a snub nose. A she-bear perhaps. A stuffed toy, much like one of Jane Harrison's totem creatures. When Tom first saw K2, it reared suddenly into view, standing out from all the other peaks around it. He was six years old. He had been scrawling pictures of it for weeks, representing the mountain that claimed his mother's body with crayon and pencil and ink, over and over again. The expedition doctor, guided by a book for children on grief, had encouraged him to express his feelings through drawings.

Tom worked hungrily and impatiently through the book. When asked to draw the different ways people die, his first pictures showed guns and bullets, knives and drowning. Only later did he produce a careful drawing of his mother and only after he finished it did he show how she died: the pyramid of the mountain was dramatically outlined on the page, followed by heavy strokes of black pencil representing the storm. He returned to this image again and again. He often had tantrums. One night he left the mess tent after dinner and disappeared for half an hour into the darkness alone. When he returned he told his dad that he had been thinking about his mum. When she had arrived at K2, one of the first things she had done was to send a drawing of the mountain home to the children.

Many members of the climbing community criticised Jim Ballard's decision to take his children to Pakistan to see the mountain on which Alison had died. Jim had often seemed indifferent and cold to the press, too matter-of-fact, unwilling to show his grief. Some, perhaps unfairly, speculated that the pilgrimage was a media stunt. But regardless of what prompted it, for Tom and Kate, this was an extension of their normal life, a familiar environment.

Only the cameras were trained on them and their father, a man learning how to be a single parent in the glare of the media. Without Alison, Jim Ballard promised that he would support his children in whatever career they decided to pursue and that he'd encourage them to live adventurously. In interviews, he joked that it was unlikely that Tom would become a mountaineer, because it would be difficult for a boy to follow in the footsteps of 'the greatest female climber of all time'.

Though Kate was the child who bore an uncanny resemblance to Alison as a small girl, Tom began to look more and more like his mother as he grew older: red, wind-blown cheeks, a sturdy neck, a shy, dazzling smile. Though he held her face in his own, Tom grew up with only vague memories of his mother. In interviews, he said he recalled 'hardly anything', just that she was 'kind, generous and yet very determined'. In the first years of his life, he would have witnessed Alison returning triumphant from the great north faces of the Alps, coming back to their campsite in time to put him and his sister to bed, or play with them in the snow. He travelled to the Himalaya and got used to camping in harsh conditions. Mountains were a fundamental part of Alison and Jim's relationship and they were guiding spirits in their parenting too. Tom had tasted life in the mountains. And when Alison was dead, mountains remained proud between them, a jagged connection. They were the keepers of his mother's body. He could not blame them for her death, because you can't blame ice and solemn crevasses, weathered rock and scree. You can't blame the sky the mountains touch, the clouds and the freezing nights. He later said:

> I know how much I am connected to the mountains. And how much I love them. So I understand very clearly why she went there and how she was killed doing something that she loved. I mean, you can't really ask for more than that, can you? I far prefer that she died doing something that she loved and which was her life and her passion, rather than living for years with some terrible lingering sickness.

I find it painful to think of Tom and Kate as teenagers. The milestones of their childhood – secondary school, birthdays, adolescence – all passed without their mother there. As a teen, Tom attended school sporadically, preferring to get out into the hills around Fort William when the weather allowed. Despite this, he was articulate and talented, good at most things he turned his hand to. He was always described as intelligent and quick-witted as well as stubborn and determined. He understood the nuanced ethics of climbing and believed passionately in showing reverence for environments. To talk of 'conquering' a mountain was ridiculous in his eyes. We do not conquer anything, least of all a landscape subject to unpredictable weather conditions, freak storms and dangers. It is luck that allows some to succeed. Tom was emphatic: 'I don't really see why we have the word "conquering" in the English language.'

As a young man, his favourite book was T.E. Lawrence's sprawling epic *Seven Pillars of Wisdom*, the inspiration for *Lawrence of Arabia*. Though not a climbing narrative, Tom was drawn to its depiction of the adventurous spirit, embodied in the book's most often-quoted passage:

> All men dream: but not equally. Those who dream by night in the dusty recesses of their minds wake in the day to find that it was vanity: but the dreamers of the day are dangerous men, for they may act their dream with open eyes, to make it possible.

There is no doubt that Tom recognised himself as a dreamer of the day, daring to bring his desires and ambitions into the light. As such, he was also branding himself a 'dangerous man'. His sister and father described him as serious but with a childlike sense of humour, constantly exploring. Like his mother, Tom cultivated his aptitude for solo climbing, relying only on himself. From 2002 to 2007, he did over a thousand new bouldering problems in Scotland and produced a bouldering guide to Glen Nevis, the area closest to where the family lived. The book received positive reviews.

In 2009, he returned to the Eiger, the mountain he'd climbed in utero with Alison. He planned to make the first solo ascent of the Scottish Pillars, a rarely repeated route from 1970 on the left side of the north face. He spent a season living with Jim and Kate in a barn in nearby Alpiglen in Grindelwald. Nasty weather limited his progress with the route, but eventually he soloed the whole thing piecemeal, in stages, finishing the top section in late spring 2009. He returned to free-climb Scottish Pillars in one go, then he established a new route of his own beside it, a line he named Seven Pillars of Wisdom, celebrating his beloved book and its hallowed, risky spirits. Over the next seven years, Tom and Jim were nomads, living out of a white Volkswagen van, travelling around Europe, chasing conditions in the Alps, mending tattered gear and surviving on Jim's modest pension, brewing endless cups of strong tea to pass the time. Kate was living independently by then, having qualified as a ski instructor. It was just father and son. Or father, son and mountains.

The relationship was intense, the living situation surely at times claustrophobic. They were drawn to Italy, to the daunting spindles of the Dolomites. It is easy to see why. When I was a child, Italian mountains seemed archetypal, sketches of what perfect spires should look like. Castles. Jagged fortresses. The mountains are often photographed rising above glassy, placid lakes, their image held steady in the water, water admiring rock and rock admiring itself. The prospects are imposing, the rock quality often poor. Tom was undeterred, climbing hundreds of routes, many of them free solos. He approached it with the cheerful nonchalance of someone setting out for their desk job every morning.

In those days, his climbing was fluid, prolific and, though he was extraordinarily gifted, many of his activities went under the public radar. Perhaps it was to do with the media's lingering suspicion of his father's choices, perhaps it was because Tom didn't shout loudly about his achievements. Perhaps it was because he gravitated towards the esoteric and the obscure. His particular talent was for dry-tooling, an often-overlooked aspect of the sport where climbers use axes and other gear on rock, emulating winter climbing but in totally different conditions. I have only tried dry-tooling once in Cambridge out of necessity, the Fens so monotonous that any vertical wall seemed exciting. I went with my friend Abinand to an old railway bridge in Fen Ditton, walking for miles along busy roads to get there, passing close to the A14 and turning off into a village with a glass-fronted chip shop. When we reached the bridge, we had to scramble down a bank and pick our way through brambles and forest, single file, rucksacks snagging on branches. Our reward was a small arch, graffiti plastered and crumbling, grooves in one wall where we could lodge our axes and try to swing upwards, legs dangling beneath us. I can't remember the movements now, only foxgloves and abandoned shopping trolleys and the noise of the motorway. I only encountered dry-tooling again years later when Andrew took part in a national indoor competition in Manchester. He sent me photos of men and women hauling themselves up plastic and wood, artificial overhangs. In one of them, Tom Ballard's face is at the front of the picture, keenly observing from the audience, waiting to take his turn.

Dry-tooling suited Tom's remarkable core strength, the power in his shoulders. It also helped him to train for Alpine ascents. He was particularly skilled at climbing roofs, huge imposing lids of rock which look insurmountable, and require the climber to be horizontal most of the time. By 2012, Tom had made the second ascent of the hardest dry-/mixed-tooling route in the world, Ironman, a gruelling climb in Eptingen, Switzerland. Ironman is hidden in a forest glen, something fairy-tale about it. The route itself looks crumpled, silver ledges dense with texture.

Though Tom managed impressive repeats of routes forged by others, his crowning achievement came years later with a new route in a Dolomite cave in the Marmolada, a huge, wide roof with big reaches. Tom named the cave 'Tomorrow's World' and the climb 'A Line Above the Sky'. The route is blank and steep, mainly horizontal, demands 45 metres of shoulder-straining moves. Normally, routes in caves involve a gentler introduction up the side of the cave before approaching the roof. A Line Above the Sky is sustained, turning the climber upside down, snowy mountains visible in the background. It is a dramatic, daunting prospect. When he repeated it, climber Liam Foster described A Line Above the Sky as an aesthetic delight, the best dry-tooling route he'd ever done. When I look at pictures of it, it looks as if the cave is trying to tip the climber off. Unlikely. Gravity-defying. Above all, bold.

In the photographs of him taken at that time, Tom is tanned and muscular. His eyes have a meltwater sparkle. His posture is relaxed, his smile open. He looks like a man at the height of his powers, full of daring. His expression is confident, determined: he is someone on the brink of historical achievement. He is ready for his greatest challenge. He has forgotten the boy who wanted to be encircled by his mother, Brown Bear dangling from one hand, fur worn from hugs.

/\/\/\/\/\/\/\/\/\/\/\ VIEW

When you're on rock, time doesn't stand still. Instead, it seems to move at the same speed you do, keep pace with you until you become one body, one mass. Not fluid, but purposeful. When time climbs beside you, inside you, you could be anywhere. On the crux of a roof in Sikati Cave in Kalymnos, surrounded by limestone tufa, sandy-coloured fangs, chilled by the permanent shade. You might be leaning backwards, levering yourself up, nearly horizontal, amazed that you are still moving. You could be high on Flying Buttress Direct, a sneering gritstone lip, leg raised in a heel hook, arms filling with blood. In those moments, your body is decisive, certain. It seems to climb without instruction, without need, without fear. Fear comes later. It comes in the aftermath, the calculations, the moments before the next route when not starting is still a possibility. Once you are sky-bound, moving, you are safe. Time is on your side. Time is on you, with you, in you. It is preposterous and lovely.

In those moments, you are alive the way you know a racehorse must be when its hooves strike the turf and lift and strike again, or how a bird must be in the seconds after it leaves the branch, or a plant as it opens to the sun, grateful and guarded. You are in your element. There is nothing beyond your field of vision. Nothing exists except what you can touch and hold and stand on. You become a part of the air, unremarkable, leaving no trace. It's only afterwards that you become aware of your breathing, of how slippery the rock was, how the wind threatened to peel you from the crag. Grey skies, unmoved by you. The rock asking, *What would you do for me? How much do you love me? What would you give to feel like this for ever?*

NAKED MOUNTAIN

'Mountains are not fair or unfair, they are just dangerous.'

– Reinhold Messner

2019

Tom is an elusive presence. There are no books, no diaries, few interviews in which to search for him. He is seen from a distance, climbing into the blue. Perhaps that was deliberate, a need for privacy and simplicity competing with the need to publicise his achievements. The only film ever made about Tom while he was alive follows him as he sets out to climb the great north faces of the Alps, following in his mother's footsteps and even using her old ice axes. He called his project

'Starlight and Storm', a nod to Gaston Rébuffat. It was an attempt to gain sponsorship and shine a spotlight on his climbing achievements. Alison soloed the faces in summer, Tom would do it in a single winter. It would be a new take on his mother's feat, and a far more perilous one. His father reckoned it would 'probably be impossible'. It was not. Amid the dizzying panoramas and intense close-ups in *TOM*, we hear his voice, cutting through the Alpine silence, his soft half-Italian accent: 'Soloing is a very selfish thing to do. The way it involves and isolates the people closest to you.'

The film affords Tom a strange immortality. On the face of the Cima Grande di Lavaredo, gloriously alone, Tom seems at home. His hair is thick, brown, streaked with lighter strands where the mountain sun has bleached it. There's something playful about him, his lips often curling into a smile, his speech deadpan, but he also seems uncomfortable in front of the camera. He particularly dislikes having his photo taken. His eyes are intense, pooled, greenish blue. He makes definite movements with his hands and often looks into the distance. His walk is confident. There is a solidity to him – mountain-like – but also a shyness. In company, he often seems playful and amused, though he just as often turns inward, changing as a mountain changes, altered by internal weather. It's easy to reverse-engineer his man's face and see the child so often pictured with Alison Hargreaves, determined and thatch-haired, clutching his favourite toy. I wonder if, for him, climbing was an extension of play, tinged with a strange kind of security, a memory of the summers he spent on campsites in the Alps while his mother was in the mountains.

The film catches something of his boldness. On his first north face attempt, Tom reached the top in darkness after a solo in windy conditions. As the light failed, he realised he had forgotten his headlamp and couldn't find the descent route. He was forced to bivvy without adequate clothing, sleeping on his rope beneath a small overhang. During the night he got frostbite on his toes. After descending the next morning, he was taken straight to hospital. It could have been an abrupt end to Starlight and Storm. But Tom was lucky. The frostbite wasn't severe. Once he'd recovered, he was able to take on the Cassin Route on the Piz Badile, then on to the Matterhorn, the Grandes Jorasses, the Petit Dru and the north face of the Eiger. He climbed the Heckmair route at lightning speed, taking just over five hours and only using fixed ropes to pull on at the legendary Hinterstoisser Traverse. His jubilance at reaching the top of all six summits was only marred by his descent, discovering a lost glove, then a shattered helmet, then the dead body of a skier. Over 20 years earlier, Alison had also encountered a corpse on the Eiger. It was Tom's first sighting of a dead body and it turned him inward, made him shudder, gripped by the seriousness of his climb and the eerie déjà vu of repeating Alison's experience decades before.

Tom always denied the influence his mother had on his climbing, even to his Italian girlfriend, Stefania Pederiva. But in 2010, when he was just 21, Tom had proposed an attempt on K2 in winter, climbing Alison's last mountain. The funding for the expedition never came and he was forced to direct his energy elsewhere. The urge to stand on the summit where his mother had stood still nagged at him. And in some interviews, he made more of a concession to her influence: 'When I was young growing up at school, I always said I would climb these mountains for her,' Ballard said in an interview with the *Telegraph*. 'But then I realised that was a little bit silly because she had already climbed them herself. I was only doing it for myself – every day I go out there is for me. Unconsciously, she is one of the reasons why I wanted to do it – but only one of the reasons.'

When I watch Tom, I imagine the camera panning out until his strong, confident body is just a dot. Small as an egg in the womb. Then, with my eyes half shut, I see all the scenes the camera doesn't show. Tom carrying his rucksack through Pakistan and staring up at the sheer sides of Nanga Parbat, 'Naked Mountain', the ridged, fluid shape of it like a newt diving into water. Tom in a blue down jacket, smiling at the camera with his ambitious, driven climbing partner, Daniele Nardi, their gear packed for a winter attempt on the Mummery Rib. After that, there are no more images. Only the speechlessness of snow, only wind lifting spindrift as it combs across the mountain, a hand ruffling a boy's hair.

After Alfie turns one, I take him to the Climbing Works, the cavernous building that had terrified me in my pregnancy, given me visions of my child falling into space with nothing to hold him. The Mini Works is a cheerful cave of a room with a special wooden slide and miniature climbing shoes. The sessions for toddlers are called

Rock Tots, led by an angular, friendly climber with blonde dreadlocks down to her waist. Alfie is dwarfed by even the smallest wall, but he is thrilled to be in its presence. He stares up at the multicoloured holds, some smooth discs, some jagged and protruding. He totters around, stepping up on the footholds and stepping down again. He jumps clean off the edge of one of the padded mats and lands in front of a surprised grandmother. Most of the children here are bigger, three years old at least. Alfie is wearing blue dungarees with cartoon polar bears on them and I wonder if it is a bad omen to dress your son in an emblem of extinction on his first climbing session.

The instructor brings over a basket stuffed with tiny teddy bears and other cuddly toys and lets Alfie plunge his arm in. He selects a red monkey with one eye missing. Then she mimics climbing with it, hopping the toy up the wall from hold to hold, tucking it behind a neon-purple grip just out of Alfie's reach. Her movements are poised and purposeful. Alfie soon gets the idea. His steps are jerky and unbalanced, but he gets his feet up onto a jutting orange ledge and perches there in his little blue boots with the red laces. She steadies him, then takes her hands away and he manages the next move on his own. I am amazed by the instinct to cling, to ascend, how naturally he seems to be drawn upwards, even if he can't climb yet. The holds are lollipop bright and he wants to stroke them. When he grabs the monkey, he is delighted and we applaud. Next to us, an older boy has learned that boulder 'problems' involve sticking to holds of the same colour. He shimmies his way to the top using only pink holds and Alfie stares after him. Later, when it is quiet and I think nobody is looking, I hoist Alfie to the top of the slab and climb up behind, steadying him with one hand so he can't fall. I crouch on top and cuddle him close, looking down at the space below us. We go down the slide together, me clutching him. He's bored now and tired, flinging his limbs around with abandon, demanding malt loaf and juice.

We sit together by the bags and eat apples, Alfie munching on the core of his. I love his momentary stillness, the chance to lean against him and breathe in his biscuity scent. He is already outrunning me, no longer the baby who clung to my warm skin and asked for me through the night. We watch the children climb and I watch the eager parents, studying their faces for signs of concern. Most of them offer encouragement to the kids, their voices level. One scrolls her phone as her daughter turns cartwheels on the mat. Alfie is mesmerised by movements and height, craning his neck to watch the climbers. I know that when I read enjoyment on his face and in his small limbs, I'm partly projecting something, a need for him to be bold and intrepid, transfixed by height. I have brought him here because it is what I want for him but also what I fear.

I think of the playground behind the White Hart pub in Calow, how the beer garden ran down to the rutted, churned-up farm fields, the woods beyond. My dad bent over the crossword with his pint of session ale and the white-blonde-haired girl who asked me if he was my grandad. The monkey bars I tried to swing from to impress him and how I plummeted down to meet the wood chipping, almost breaking my arm. The ache of it and the scent of pine, mud in my hair. I think of the posters in our living room, panoramic views of Skye and Torridon. The walking magazines spilling from the shelves. The rucksack my dad packed neatly before each trip, ticking everything off on a list, page filled with his slanted handwriting. The log book he kept, recording every Munro I climbed. I think of the first Scottish summits I ever stood on with him and how he pointed out the hills on every side, knowing the mountains by name. How keenly I followed him, how proud I felt when he told me about climbs he did before I was born. Like Alison Hargreaves, mountains were part of my family. Ridges ran between us and we talked across them, gleeful, sharing a common language. And like Alison, mountains are part of my mothering, part of what I want to pass on to my son, sharing the exhilaration I first tasted when I bent my head to a freezing mountain stream, smelling sheep shit and ferrous sweat and bracken.

Ever since he was born, I have dreamed of Alfie climbing with me, of the bothies we'll stay in and the paths we'll find, late-night campfire suppers and morning flapjacks, the stink of insect repellent and the burn of blisters. I have imagined teaching him to map-read, plotting routes with him, buying him his first rock shoes and belay device. I have even pictured belaying him on a top rope, watching him scamper up gritstone, scraping his knees and elbows, proud and breathless and undeterred. I am invested in his wildness, smiling when he brings me huge chunks of rock and calls them 'pretty', loving his stubborn refusal to be lifted out of streams, his determination to find the deepest part he can and stand in it, the current whirling around him. When he finds the path of most resistance, or careers down a slope, or crawls his way through brambles to occupy a den built for older boys, I encourage him. Once on a walk in the Peak District, I turned around to find he'd scrambled up to the top of a rock without me noticing. I was strangely calm, unafraid of the height. I celebrate his confidence. But beneath it all, there's a more subtle current of dread, an underground stream. I cannot find words for it, because naming it would tighten its grip. It is something to do with inheritance, something to do with solitude, the part of me that stays for one more drink, or walks home alone, or swims a little further out to sea than I should. I am afraid of my own vanity, this desire to shape my son in my image and my dad's image, the morose silences that also form his inheritance, the bubbling anger, the desire to outrun something nameless. I am afraid that he will climb past me, out of sight, with movements I recognise too well, movements that are my own.

*

The core of Tom's desired mountain, Nanga Parbat, is a long ridge, a huge bulk of ice and rock, trending southwest–northeast. In 1895, British mountaineer Alfred Mummery led an expedition to attempt its central spur, a reptilian spine. He never came back. The route which bears his name rises above the Diamir Glacier, climbing formidably to almost 7,000 metres and a crevassed plateau. The Mummery Rib is beautiful and awe-inspiring, an altar to nature's volatility. Reinhold Messner's brother Günther died close to the rib in 1970 as they descended nearby. The whole mountain is a crucible of wind in winter.

Sandy Allan, who, along with his climbing partner Rick Allen, made the first complete ascent of the Mazeno Ridge in 2012, likens being in its presence to witnessing the full orchestra of Nanga Parbat: the drumroll of seracs falling, the music of shifting and unstable ground. To attempt the Mummery Rib in winter is fraught with avalanche risk. Simone Moro called it 'a game of Russian roulette'. Yet that was the objective Tom and his partner Daniele Nardi had chosen. Nardi had previously climbed there with Elisabeth Revol, reaching 6,450 metres in 2015. His obsession with the route was well known. But after his climb with Revol, Nardi struggled to find climbing partners willing to face the dangers with him. Then he met Tom. And Tom was unafraid.

Nardi and Ballard had met in 2017, after Tom and his sister had returned to Pakistan, reliving the trip they made there in pilgrimage to their mother as children. Kate trekked and Tom climbed. Tom joined up with a group of Italian climbers – including Nardi – and attempted unclimbed Link Sar. They failed and barely escaped with their lives after a brush with falling seracs which missed them 'by a whisker'. They went on to establish a new rock route together. Their friendship was well established by the time Nardi mentioned the Mummery Rib.

Nardi had already climbed five 8,000-metre peaks by then. But Tom's participation in the Nanga Parbat expedition raised eyebrows in the climbing community: despite his track record as an alpinist, he had never been above 6,000 metres before. As Michael Levy observed: 'Going straight to an 8,000er was like skipping several grades in school – feasible for the preternaturally gifted, but even then not without its pitfalls.' But Nardi had tempted him with the promise of his first taste of climbing 8,000-metre peaks. The gauntlet had been thrown down. They set off into mountain air on Christmas Day 2018 and trekked to the village of Ser. Setting up camps, their tents were often buried by snow. Tom could barely make it through a chapter of *Seven Pillars of Wisdom* in his sleeping bag before his fingers became too cold to turn the pages. They dry-tooled on boulders to keep fit and waited for good weather. When they tried to make progress up the mountain, they were often thwarted by conditions, just as Alison was on her last trip to K2. Tom kept a blog for his sponsor Montane where he wrote that they had turned back from camp 1 because of a bad feeling, an instinct: 'Well-founded as a huge avalanche engulfed our line of ascent shortly after.' Frustrated by inactivity, Tom's last blog post read: 'The hardest part of an expedition is the waiting.'

On 24 February, Nardi and Tom reported to their ground team that they'd reached 6,300 metres. They added carefully, 'The weather is not good, there is fog, sleet and wind gusts.' Nardi told his Italian sponsors that they were descending to a portaledge to escape the stormy conditions. In a call later that day he said they planned to retreat further, down to camp 3 at 5,700 metres. Then satellite and radio communication with the pair went ominously silent.

Tom's girlfriend, Stefania, had been anxious about his attempt on the Mummery Rib from the very outset. She begged him not to go, something she'd never done before with any other expedition. When he was on the mountain, she texted him on 22 February: *Not happy you're climbing. It's dangerous.* He replied: *If you don't like it, leave me.* It was the last exchange the couple had – Tom disappeared two days later.

When climbers vanish, there is always brief hope, always the belief they might be found. We have been fed tales of unlikely survival, of Joe Simpson hauling himself to safety in the Andes after falling into a crevasse and breaking bones. These are the stories that we cling to. In the days following Tom's disappearance, an international rescue effort began. When Basque climber Alex Txikon helicoptered over from K2 to aid the search, he was unnerved by the volatile conditions on Nanga Parbat.

I watched the story unfold through the ghoulish light of my phone at 3am and 4am and 5am, hunched on a sofa, breastfeeding three-month-old Alfie. Each time Alfie cried and I stumbled out of bed to soothe him, I'd check Twitter obsessively, or pore over BBC articles, waiting to hear fresh news. I texted friends before dawn, sharing links to

Tom's disappearance. I received little back. They thought my curiosity morbid. Why should I care? It was none of my business. But I could not look away. On 5 March, Txikon flew a drone over Nanga Parbat and spotted two bodies in a maze of diagonal rock bands at around 5,800 metres. The bodies were roped up, within 10 feet of one another, one contorted on the slope.

Tom did not keep a diary like his mother. Other than his brief blog posts, there is no record of his final climb. Whatever his body wrote on the mountain has been erased, blown over, blanketed by fresh snow.

/\/\/\/\/\/\/\/\/\/\/\

DESCENT ROUTE

When she is safe too, when the belay has been de-rigged and the gear clipped back into place, you coil the ropes together like any pair should, any efficient team. She takes the blue rope and you take the yolk-bright yellow. The blue is always tangling of its own accord, contorting itself into improbable loops. It requires patience, demands full attention. She pays it out first, letting it run through her hands, smoothing it until it lies in a squiggle on the floor, a child's first doodle.

You have already found the mid-point of the yellow and are using your arm span to measure out coils of rope. It is satisfying, this process. Methodical. Next, you'll put it around your neck to gather the sections together, then wrap the last bits of rope around the centre, stow it in the top of your rucksack. She is slow with the blue, her movements exaggerated, almost melancholy. It is as if she wants to memorise the shape of it. She only looks up when she's fastened it untidily and crammed it into her bag. Wind has nudged the clouds out to sea. There is a patch of clear sky over you both. The door to an attic you could climb into. As you turn to descend, the sun lets down its ladder for a moment, then retracts it.

All the waiting, all the belaying, has made you chill off. You stop to put on another layer, a soft down jacket. You pull the hood up over your head and it muffles the world so at first you don't hear her when she speaks.

'Thanks. Thank you for that.'

You grin. 'The old ones are the best.'

'Does that apply to people?'

You smirk, but she can't see you. The steepness of the path demands you keep single file, scuttle over the loose rocks. With every movement, you are eroding the face of Great Langdale. You have always known this in an abstract sense, but today you feel the attrition beneath your boots, notice it. The earth is dense and heavy, but it is not fixed. Every step, every climb, makes a difference. This is the valley accepting you, letting you pass, taking your imprint. She is a few metres ahead of you. She looks small underneath her huge backpack, furtive.

You think perhaps you will always remember her like this: unspeaking, hemmed by weak sun, hurrying slightly in the cold. Her knees braced against the gradient, muscles working to keep her upright. She has her hair stuffed into a knitted hat and the bobble almost bounces as she walks. It is faintly comical.

When you reach the wider track, you look back at the buttress you've left, a reflex. It has forgotten you. She looks at you kindly.

'I don't know if I'll come back here. My knees don't like it any more.'

If you wanted to fold her in your arms, you could, rucksack and all. You could pick her up so easily.

Instead you say, 'Pint, Mum?'

At the Old Dungeon Ghyll, you hold the door open for her, but she's dawdling in the car park, looking at the Pikes. You go in without her. You sink into your chair and wait.

HER OWN IMAGE

Somewhere in the heaven
Of lost futures
The lives we might have lived
Have found their own fulfilment.

– Derek Mahon

2021

When I was in the last stages of writing this book, hunched at a desk in the front room, a man I knew, an acquaintance, someone I'd not quite known long enough to call a friend yet, knocked at our front door. He seemed agitated. He invited himself in, bringing cold and diamonds of rain, said he needed to talk to me while my son was at nursery. My pulse quickened. Sit down, he said. I almost fell backwards. My heartbeat was so loud in my skull I almost couldn't hear what he was saying.

Unaccountably, I thought of how news of a death is delivered, how a climbing accident is reported to relatives. I saw Jim Ballard again, at home in Fort William in 1995, the receiver pressed to his ear. I thought of him replacing the handset and beginning the long walk to the next room. Then I thought of Tom's death, the moment his body was seen in the snow, the person who had to translate that into a message that could be communicated. I heard the thrum of the rescue helicopters. I knew Alfie was safe at pre-school, covering his hands in paint and making messy prints of trees, or singing along to an alphabet song, miming the actions faithfully. But I could not shake the instinct that something must have happened to him. I was dizzy and nauseous, the room beginning to cartwheel around me. I sat among my son's toys, his beloved marble run and his stash of fat cuddly animals and searched for something to hold on to.

'There's no easy way to say this. We've found images of you – or someone who looks exactly like you – on a porn site.'

I laughed. I was hysterical, relieved, giddy. Then I doubled over and sobbed.

Hours later, I sat at my partner's computer reviewing the photographs with a forensic eye. Again, I thought of bodies at the site of accidents, the crumpled shapes that Alison Hargreaves must have passed on her way to the summit of Everest, contorted with their final efforts, preserved by cold. I thought of her own body which was never brought home. Of Tom and his climbing partner, buried by weather. I was not looking at myself exactly. Here were scenes of violence, exact and pornographic. These bodies being doubly penetrated, violated with fists and objects, held down and tied up were not mine. But from each one my face was smiling, eyes fixed on the camera, teeth bared. In some images, my tattoos had been juxtaposed onto the woman's body. And some were entirely realistic: a photograph of me being strangled by a muscled, grimacing man, the workings of Photoshop invisible. As I clicked on each photo, bypassing the comments asking for me to be humiliated, abused and violated, I looked into my own eyes. It was incongruous: these were taken from holiday pictures on my social media profiles and I looked radiant, cheerful. We call the eyes windows to the soul. I felt as if I was made from broken glass.

Whoever took my images and turned them into deepfake pornography – an act which, at the time, wasn't a crime under UK law – wanted to see me humiliated. Their means of doing so was to remind me that, as a woman, you can always be reduced to an object of sexual gratification, sexual violence. In those pictures, I was not a writer, not a climber, not a mother, not a partner or friend. I was simply flesh.

The concept of the deepfake fascinates me: in some images, technology is used to simulate a naked photo from a clothed photo. The pornographic gaze is like an X-ray, removing all the things the female subject might project into the world before them, their words and actions, their achievements and opinions. Deepfake technology is new, but this kind of gaze is not. As John Berger writes in *Ways of Seeing* (1972), a 'woman's self [is] split into two':

> A woman must continually watch herself. She is almost continually accompanied by her own image of herself . . . And so she comes to consider the

> surveyor and the surveyed within her as the two constituent yet always distinct elements of her identity as a woman.

This is not just about visuals, about pictures and film. This surveillance lives in words and actions, writing and gossip, silence and laughter. When Alison Hargreaves was criticised in the press as a bad mother, she had her image, her surveyed image, thrust back at her, magnified. After she climbed Everest, Nigella Lawson in *The Times* accused her of a 'reality-denying self-centredness'. And after her loss, Polly Toynbee compared climbing to drug-taking, adding 'what is interesting about Alison Hargreaves is that she behaved like a man'. Her friend Alison Osius reflected sadly:

> Hargreaves was public property; her death, news round the world. It was especially painful to women climbers, many of whom had been trying to sort out their own conflicting obligations to self and family . . . Some thought and wondered, well, had she been selfish? But we cannot judge that. We can only draw our own lines.

In being a mountaineer, Alison tried to unify the contradictory aspects of herself, turn them into pure power, pure movement, pure attention. I find this unity in writing, Alison found it in the hills. And even as an amateur climber, I understand how mountains can simplify your existence, give the sense of presence and focus that I find on the page. The response to her death was to divide her again, remind her of the split nature of womanhood, foreground the image. Male mountaineers are allowed to become something other, something essential, when they climb: they become an agent, a climber. Female mountaineers strive to be climbers too, but society does not allow them to escape their prefix. They are still mothers in the mountains, or childless women who are yet to become mothers, or childless women who haven't fulfilled their biological destiny.

When I won the women's category in a local fell race in Derbyshire as a young woman, I was given a set of Perspex casserole dishes as my first prize while the male category winner received a cash prize. Over the years, this has become an anecdote I tell at parties, but my laughter is always slightly bitter. In giving me the dishes, the organisers were reminding me of my duality, my responsibilities.

A container with a lid on it. I have become used to it: in another fell race where I set a new women's record, the announcer at the prize ceremony revealed each of the male category winners first, from youths to veterans, and let them pick from an array of gifts – hi-tech gear and bottles of whisky. By the time it was my turn, I was left with a pair of socks. I picked them up and fixed my face in a smile, an expression of gratitude. It seemed important to be polite, to be thankful. Surveyor and surveyed. I can never just be a runner, as I can never just be a writer. At literary events, I will be reminded of my femaleness, receive unwanted approaches from male writers, have my clothes and hair and make-up observed, my subject matter interrogated. *Write about your body. Write more poems about children. Don't write so many poems about children.* Alison was always seen as a mother-mountaineer by the public, not just a climber. This reflects the painful duality of her life and death, her constant sense of being pulled in two directions, wanting the children and wanting K2. But it is a double burden to carry.

In the weeks after I discovered the pornographic fakes online, I felt detached. It was difficult to run, climb or lift weights. I was always vigilant, watching myself as if from afar, as if I were a small creature in a vast landscape and I could holler to myself if a threat emerged. Frightened rabbit. I had dreams about walking through subways and tunnels with two huge men blocking the light at the other side. No way out and no way through, nothing to do but keep walking towards them, towards a hand forced over my mouth and my back forced against a wall, a knife pressed against my throat. In some of these dreams I had a huge dog to protect me, a pit bull straining in a spiked collar and chain, but the men shot or stabbed it as I howled with anguish.

My way out of this trap was writing. In speaking publicly about my experience, I was able to take back control, reassert my right to speak without shame. I posted a video in which I addressed my tormentor and said that I was not humiliated, merely bored: bored of objectification, bored of the corners of the internet I'd had to visit to get my image taken down, bored of Twitter trolls and walking quickly in the street. Slowly, the nightmares abated. Instead of dreaming of rape, I began to dream of climbing walls. In my most vivid dream, I was watching my teenage stepdaughter bouldering at an indoor gym, guiding her from the ground, suggesting foot placements. She was lithe and confident and I applauded her, told her she had a rare talent. When I watched her, it was like watching the air find its form. I woke up resolved to take her out to Burbage and let her explore. She is just 14. She spends her days inside the lit square of her smartphone. But she is nostalgic about lake swims and ill-fated muddy walks, the single time I took her to a climbing wall and let her lose herself in its puzzles and expressions. I am a mother to a son, but I am also part role model to a teenager. In a world that judges her by the colour of her hair, her skin, the shade of her foundation, the length of her skirt, it feels like a crushing responsibility.

The story of your motherhood or childlessness is not just your own. It is the story of your mother, your grandmother, your great-grandmother, all the women who came before you and the others who surround you, who mesh their lives with your own. It is the story of all the women you are connected to and their thwarted desires, their split selves, their subjectivity. My story is the story of a woman who despaired of me in a multi-storey car park, who smelled of soap and lily of the valley, who told me stories when I was sick and cupped my feverish head in my hands and sobbed with joy and relief when her grandson was born. It is the story of her mother who was so skinny when she gave birth she barely looked pregnant, who spent the prime of her life in a TB sanatorium, defended her brother with her fists, cooked me breakfasts before school. It is the story of my great-grandmother, still witty and sharp at 95 years old, soft-spoken, survivor of domestic abuse from a husband who committed suicide. Everything they gave me is mine to contain, mine to pass on to the younger women who surround me and who open parts of their lives to me. If women are always to be doubled, surveyor and surveyed, then let us be multiple. Let us stand so close that we seem to merge together, the dead and the living, the real and the fictional. They cannot split us because we are united, we are myriad. Women climbing with women. Women tied together on the rope. Women who invented imaginary climbing companions so that passing male climbers would leave them alone and stop offering unsolicited advice.

One day on the drive home from Mam Tor in the High Peak, a rounded hill near Castleton known as the 'mother hill' or 'Heights of the Mother', Alfie falls asleep, head lolling in his car seat, mouth slightly open. Even now, I'm always gripped by the urge to check his breathing, to place my hand on his chest and feel the reassuring rise and fall of his ribcage. It is a brilliant day now, bright and clear. When we were at Mam Tor, it was overcast and claggy, disappointing walking weather. I stop my car under Stanage Edge, at the least popular end of the crag, and sit in silence. I look across to High Neb, the buttresses and slabs, arêtes and edges, all flattened from here, unified, like the crest of a wave. It's a weekday out of season, with hardly anyone out, but I can see two shapes moving, a flash of colour from a fleece.

I let my head fall back against the car headrest. I shut my eyes for a second, as if the view is too much for me. It's then that I see them, mother and son, climbing methodically with the winter sun on their backs. He is broad-shouldered and strong, she is short but just as powerful. Sometimes she leads and he pays out the rope for her. Sometimes he leads and she follows. Below them, the Hope Cement Works plume with smoke, the reservoirs are flat coins. A grouse calls sharply. The rock is cold, the friction is excellent. Alison squints into the light. In quiet, suburban houses below, people are still making breakfast, packing school lunches, drinking endless cups of tea. They have started out early. She knows they have all the time they need.

Notes on sources

This book quotes extensively from *Regions of the Heart: The Triumph and Tragedy of Alison Hargreaves* (Penguin, 2000) with permission from the authors, David Rose and Ed Douglas.

I have also quoted from and drawn from Jim Ballard's account of the trip he made with Tom and Kate to Pakistan in *One and Two Halves to K2* (BBC Books, 1996).

I have been hugely influenced by and quoted from Maria Coffey's book *Where the Mountain Casts Its Shadow: The Dark Side of Extreme Adventure* (Arrow Books, 2004) and by her book *Explorers of the Infinite* (Jeremy P. Tarcher / Penguin, 2008).

Lines from 'Love' by Philip Larkin are excerpted from *Collected Poems* (Faber & Faber, 2008).

Lines from 'The Good Neighbour' by John Burnside (from *The Good Neighbour*, 2005) are reproduced by kind permission of the author and Jonathan Cape.

Lines from 'The Gift' by Li-Young Lee are excerpted from *Rose* (BOA Editions Ltd, 1986) www.boaeditions.org

'Fire and Ice', from *The Collected Poems* by Robert Frost © 1969 Holt Rinehart and Winston, Inc., published by Vintage Books. Extract reproduced by permission of The Random House Group Ltd

The quote from Gwen Moffat in 'First Ledge' is taken from her memoir *Space Below My Feet* (Quality Book Club, 1961).

Lines in 'Vertigo' are taken from *Bluets* by Maggie Nelson (Jonathan Cape, 2017).

'Dreamers of the Day' draws on material from 'Finding Tom Ballard' by Michael Levy (Ascent, 2020).

Lines from 'Sky Birth' by Liz Berry are excerpted from *The Republic of Motherhood* (Chatto & Windus, 2018).

Lines from 'The Winter Climbing' by Andrew Greig are excerpted from *This Life, This Life: New & Selected Poems 1970-2006* (Bloodaxe Books, 2006).

Lines from 'Leaves' by Derek Mahon (from *The Poems: 1961-2020*, 2021) are reproduced by kind permission of The Estate of Derek Mahon and The Gallery Press, www.gallerypress.com

Lines from the novel *Climbers* by M. John Harrison (Gollancz, 2013) are included with kind permission from the author.

'The Last Swim' by Michael Laskey (from *The Man Alone: New and Selected Poems,* 2008) is reproduced by kind permission of the author and Smith/Doorstop.

'Vertigo' quotes from Francis Sanzaro's article 'Are Mountain Climbers Selfish' (*New York Times*, 27 April 2019). https://www.nytimes.com/2019/04/27/opinion/mountain-climbing.html

'Carrying a Heart' quotes from Jemima Diki Sherpa's piece 'Everest's deadly demands: a Sherpa's view', (*Financial Times*, 2 May 2014). https://www.ft.com/content/e9734a50-cef4-11e3-9165-00144feabdc0

'Dreamers of the Day' quotes from 'A Note from Alex Honnold's Mom' by Dierdre Wolownick (*Climbing*, 23 May 2016). https://www.climbing.com/people/a-note-from-alex-honnolds-mom/

'Dreamers of the Day' also quotes from Robert Chalmers 'Tom Ballard, mountaineer, never wanted to die in bed' (*GQ*, 9 March 2019). https://www.gq-magazine.co.uk/article/tom-ballard-climber

Other references and further recommended reading

Clouds from Both Sides by Julie Tullis with Peter Gillman (Vertebrate, 2017)

In Some Lost Place: The First Ascent of Nanga Parbat's Mazeno Ridge by Sandy Allan (Vertebrate, 2016)

Winter 8000: Climbing the World's Highest Mountains in the Coldest Season by Bernadette McDonald (Vertebrate, 2020)

The Sharp End of Life: A Mother's Story by Dierdre Wolownick (Mountaineers Books, 2019)

Down from the Mountain: The Life and Death of a Grizzly Bear by Bryce Andrews (Houghton Mifflin Harcourt, 2019)

Square Haunting: Five Women, Freedom and London Between the Wars by Francesca Wade (Faber & Faber, 2020)

Acknowledgements

Thank you to Robyn Drury, Matthew Turner and Clare Bullock, without whom this book would never have existed, and to Marcella Sutcliffe at the Chapelgarth Estate for allowing me 'a room of one's own'.

I am indebted to Ed Douglas and David Rose who wrote Alison's biography, *Regions of the Heart*, the guide-text for this book and for much of my life too.

Thank you to Jim Ballard and Kate Ballard for their permission to write about Alison and Tom. Thanks also to Bev England, Sandy Allan, Bernadette McDonald, David Wilson, Maria Coffey, Robert Chalmers and the committee at the Banff Mountain Film and Book Festival.

Some short extracts from this book first appeared in *Southword* journal and in 'Mother Mountain', a short documentary video published by Alexander. My thanks to the editors of both, especially Tim Martin.

Thank you to my friends and companions on the rope: Anna Fleming, Harry, Pete and the rest of the DICS, Heather Dawe, and especially Andrew Marshall, for being there through many challenges. I am also indebted to all the brilliant women who have been on the journey of new motherhood with me, all of the NCT mums, and particularly Rachel Bower.

Finally, thanks to my husband, Jess, and to Blue and Leo. And to my son, Alfie, for letting me be his rambling, imperfect mother.